MW00719823

Provincial and National Park
CAMPGROUNDS
in British Columbia
A Complete Guide

Jayne Seagrave

HERITAGE HOUSE

Copyright © 1997 Jayne Seagrave

CANADIAN CATALOGUING IN PUBLICATION DATA

Seagrave, Jayne 1961-
Provincial and National Park Campgrounds in British Columbia

ISBN 1-895811-30-9

1. Provincial parks and reserves—British Columbia—Guidebooks
2. National parks and reserves—British Columbia—Guidebooks
3. Camp sites, facilities, etc.—British Columbia—Guidebooks
4. Outdoor recreation—British Columbia—Guidebooks
5. British Columbia—Guidebooks
I. Title.
FC3813.S42 1997   917.1104'4   C97-910134-4
F1087.S42 1997

First Edition 1997

Heritage House wishes to acknowledge the support of Heritage Canada, the British Columbia Arts Council and the Cultural Services Branch of the Ministry of Small Business, Tourism and Culture and BC Parks.

Front Cover Photo: Al Nickull
Back Cover Photos: BC Parks, Jayne Seagrave, Dennis Hurd
Cover, Book Design and Typesetting: Darlene Nickull
Photos: Author's photos unless otherwise noted
Edited by: Rhonda Bailey

HERITAGE HOUSE PUBLISHING COMPANY LTD.
Unit #8 - 17921 55th Ave., Surrey, BC V3S 6C4

Printed in Canada by Freisens

Acknowledgements

The publication of this guide to national and provincial park campgrounds fulfils my five-year-long ambition to write and publish a book on camping in British Columbia. A number of individuals and organizations have helped me to achieve my goal, and I am indebted to them.

The data I collected from site visits was greatly supplemented by the valuable information and assistance I received from BC Parks—both from the headquarters in Victoria and the regional offices. I thank them for granting permission to reproduce their maps and photographs in this text. I am also grateful to Tourism BC for letting me access their maps, to Canadian Heritage Parks Canada for providing recent data on national parks, and Dennis Hurd for the use of their photographs. A special thanks to Darlene and Al Nickull for going well beyond the call of duty to provide interesting photos and help complete the book on a timely basis. Also, I thank Dave Prentice, The British Columbia Adventure Network and his excellent http://www.bcadventure.com website team for their photos. Unless identified as national parks all campgrounds are in BC provincial parks.

The enthusiasm, professional approach, advice, and expertise of the editorial staff at Heritage House assisted the quality and appearance of the text. Their ability and commitment to a tight time frame greatly helped the book's development.

The largest debt is owed to my camping partner, Andrew Dewberry, who encourages my dreams and ambitions and who taught me to camp. Without him this book would not have been possible.

Table of Contents

Alphabetical Index to Campgrounds

Introduction

This book has been written out of a love of camping and a deep respect for British Columbia (BC). As Canada's third largest province, BC covers 950,000 square kilometres of land, including 18,000 square kilometres of inland water. Larger than any US state except Alaska, BC has more land designated to provincial parks than all the state parks in the United States (excluding Alaska and Hawaii) and boasts over 400 different locations for day use and camping. In addition, six national parks are found in the province, four of these with developed camping facilities. With all this space for exploration and over 12,000 camping spots, it is little wonder that the "camping experience" has become an integral part of recreational life for BC residents and visitors alike.

The following chapters provide details of BC's national and provincial park campgrounds and have been divided into nine regions: Southwestern BC, Vancouver Island (including the Gulf Islands), Okanagan-Similkameen, High Country, Kootenay Country, Rocky Mountain, Peace River and the Alaska Highway, Cariboo Chicotin Coast, and North by Northwest. These areas mirror those used by BC Parks and Tourism BC in the free supportive literature they distribute at most tourist information centres in the province.

The introductory chapter of this guide details important background information on camping in British Columbia, including how to select a camping spot, what to take camping, the reservation process, and potential hazards. It offers guidance to the novice and acts as a reminder to the seasoned camper.

Ensuing chapters give details of the provincial and national campgrounds in each of the nine regions, their location, the facilities offered, the recreational activities available, and additional information of interest. Fortunately the number of BC parks continues to grow and develop, and as a result the information contained in these pages is subject to change. The campgrounds introduced after early 1997 are not included in this edition. While over 150 campgrounds are reviewed in detail, for a small number of campgrounds only summary information is presented. These campgrounds are often in remote locations accessible only from rough gravel roads unsuitable for many vehicles and often do not have rudimentary facilities such as fresh water. Such "primitive" campgrounds lacking in one or more of the basic facilities are briefly described at the end of each chapter.

Introduction

For those who seek guidance on their choice of campgrounds, seven-, fourteen-, and twenty-one-day camping itineraries have been constructed at the end of the book. These selections are based on my personal experiences and amenity evaluations and are designed to cover pragmatic travel distances on any given day.

The book has been written both for those who camp in tents and those who use recreational vehicles (RVs). While my own camping experience has been confined to using a tent, I am well aware that many residents and visitors to the province utilize a motor vehicle, and for this reason additional information on RV rentals, sales, and service is contained in the appendix.

Camping is a personal experience; what appeals to one person may not appeal to another. British Columbia is blessed with some of the most breathtaking scenery in the world. Many of the provincial and national parks nestle in the heart of this beauty and are yours to experience at relatively little cost. Over the course of the last six years I have travelled and camped in every region of BC and have been amazed at the stunning beauty the province offers. It still surprises me that many residents of BC do not camp. I hope this book encourages more individuals to take the plunge and use the excellent facilities provided in BC's parks. A wealth of adventures and experiences can be enjoyed by those of every age. So, what are you waiting for?

Watch for special signs at Park Entrances. (courtesy Al Nickull)

The Camping Experience

The aim of this chapter is to provide some of the basic ground rules on camping in BC's national and provincial parks. While the information in this chapter is intended primarily for the uninitiated, to show them what to expect, those who regularly camp will find the data on making reservations, what to take, bears, and other hazards serves as a useful reminder.

Arrival at a Provincial or National Park Campground

All national and provincial park campgrounds are well sign-posted from major highways. A sign (blue for provincial parks, brown for national parks) two kilometres prior to the campground turnoff is the first warning you will receive, followed by another 400 metres from the campground to direct you to the access road. The park operator will post notices on these roadside signs to state when a campground is full or closed. You will come to appreciate what a real advantage this is if the campground is located 60 kilometres from the highway on a rough gravel road.

Selecting your spot

Presuming you do not have a reservation (see below) the biggest excitement upon arrival is selecting *your* spot. Depending on the season, time of day, and location of the park, this decision may already be out of your hands. The park may be full or there may be only one place left. Some parks have areas specifically designated for tents while most have spots suitable for both RVs and tenters. A number of parks offer "double spots" ideal for two families camping together and pull-through spots for the larger RVs. A map of the campground at the entrance of the park details where these are to be found. If the park offers a reservation service the reserved sites will be listed at the park's entrance. Once you have established the restrictions, you should "cruise" the campground to select your spot. Campsites by a beach, lake, river, or creek are the most desirable locations, so head for these first, making a mental note of where the woodpile and water are located. Try to avoid areas of stagnant water (mosquito breeding grounds) or spots close to the "thunderboxes" (pit toilets) which during the park's warm summer months may exude unpleasant odors, attract flies, and offer disturbance from banging doors. At first glance, spots near the flush toilets and showers may seem convenient, but remember that between 5:00 p.m. and 11:00 p.m. and 7:00 a.m. and 11:00 a.m. most people at the campground will be visiting these facilities at least twice and walking past your site in order to do it. During these hours your privacy may be forsaken as carefree campers amble from washroom back to camping spot via your site. Alternatively, if you have children in your party or want to meet people, you may deem these to be ideal spots.

Once you have driven around and made a mental note of your preferences, return to and claim your first choice (collecting wood and water en route if you want). Should you not want to pitch camp immediately, leave just a plastic tablecloth or water jug on the picnic table to state to the world this is *your* spot. If the campground requires self-registration you need to complete a self-registration form and pin the receipt to your spot (see "Fees" below).

If you delay pitching your tent or going to collect water, remember to note when it gets dark. This is particularly relevant if you are camping in the shoulder seasons of early spring and late summer, when darkness falls as early as 7:00 p.m. Arriving at a campground late, pitching your tent in the dark, and cooking dinner by flashlight is a challenge to say the least. In contrast, relaxing by the fire while the sun goes down and the stars come out is a highly pleasurable experience when you know your bed is made, dinner is over, and the washing up done.

Exploring the vicinity

Once established in your new home, you are ready to explore the campground. The first port of call should be a return visit to the information board at the park's entrance, where you will find a full map of the campground, details of the hazards of the area, if any, lists of interpretive programs available, information about other campgrounds in the region, leaflets and maps. A number of the larger provincial parks have camp hosts. These are wonderful (usually retired) people who live for one to two months in the park and supply maps, park guides, and handouts and generally help visitors. They are an excellent source of information about the area and have a little sign by their spot telling visitors whether they are on or off duty, so you know when you can disturb them. Seldom will you mistake the hosts' spot as it is usually the most established on site, a true "home away from home." As someone who adores provincial parks, I cannot wait until I am old enough—although there is no age stipulated I have yet to meet a park host under 60—and have enough time to volunteer as a BC Provincial Park Host. (Anyone interested in becoming a park host should contact the BC Parks Regional Office of the area they would like to be assigned.)

Fees

During the early evening hours in most parks an attendant will come and collect payment (cash only). Camping fees vary depending on the facilities provided; campgrounds with showers tend to be the most expensive, whereas less developed campgrounds have lower fees. Fees include GST and in 1997 ranged from $6.00–$15.50 for provincial parks and up to $22.00 in national parks. National parks also request payment for firewood (in 1996 this was $3.00). An additional entrance fee is charged in all national parks, whether you intend to camp or not.

Provincial and National Park Campgrounds in BC

In registering you will be asked to provide your name, the number of people in your party, car registration number, and where you are from. You can pay for as many nights as you want up to a maximum of 14 nights in both provincial and national parks. A receipt displaying the date at which you intend to leave will be posted on your spot. Some parks operate an honour/self-registration system whereby you deposit the campground fee in an envelope, place it in a box at the entrance to the park, and secure a receipt. In these instances it is good to ensure you carry small bills and change, although fellow campers are usually willing to oblige. Instructions on self-registering are printed on a sign at the park's entrance and on the deposit envelope. Park attendants, like provincial park hosts, are good sources of information on weather conditions, local activities, the best fishing locations, and so on.

Residents of BC who are 65 or older may camp for half price in provincial parks up to June 14 and after Labour Day. From June 15 to Labour Day, full rates apply. Individuals with disabilities who have been issued with a BC Parks Disabled Access Pass camp for free.

Facilities

With a few exceptions, all campgrounds have the basic facilities of water, wood, pit toilets, picnic tables, and fire pits. Larger campgrounds can include sani-stations, flush toilets, showers, wheelchair access, interpretive programs, visitor's centres, and group camping. Washroom facilities are generally well maintained, clean, and unlike many campgrounds I have stayed in abroad, they never run out of toilet tissue. (Preconditioned in Europe, I took years to realize this and stop carrying a spare supply). Gravel camping spots are tidied and raked after each visitor departs, garbage is regularly collected, and overall, the facilities provided in BC's national and provincial parks are excellent.

Although some campgrounds are open throughout the year, fees for individual camping spots are collected only from April to October. I have found that, even in September, despite remaining open, many of the smaller campgrounds do not collect fees.

Look for the Information Centre when you visit a campground. (courtesy Al Nickull)

10

The Rules of Park Camping

While few formal rules exist there is a definite camping etiquette which should be observed for the benefit of all. Most of the items in the list below are common sense and serve only as a gentle reminder:

1. Quiet time starts at 11:00 p.m. when the park gates are closed. Campsite visitor restrictions apply and park gates are closed between 11:00 p.m. and 7:00 a.m.
2. In season, the threat of forest fires is immense, so extreme caution should be taken. At all times light fires only in metal fire pits.
3. Store food in your vehicle, in airtight containers. If you do not have a vehicle and are in an area frequented by bears, hang food in bags suspended on a tree branch, four metres above the ground. With 100,000 black bears in BC, this is not a rule to ignore.
4. To protect the vegetation, camp only in the designated areas.
5. Recycle as much as possible using BC Parks dispensers.
6. Take from the woodpile only what you need. One of the advantages BC parks have over national parks, private campgrounds, and those in the United States is free firewood although while I was researching this book, staff at BC Parks told me this may change in the future.
7. Checkout time is midday, and the maximum length of stay is 14 days per year in any one park. A camping party is regarded as a family from the same address, or if not a family, a maximum of four people 13 years or older of which one must be over the age of 16.
8. Cutting branches, flowers, berries, or mushrooms is prohibited in all parks. Enjoy the flora and fauna by looking, smelling, and photographing, but leave it for others to have the same pleasure.
9. Clean your campsite on departure. Remove all garbage.
10. Keep pets on a leash in campgrounds and all other restricted areas.
11. Do not use your fire pit for garbage disposal. Partly burnt food tempts wildlife, and blackened beer cans are an annoyance.
12. BC Parks allows only one camping vehicle per site. The only exception is when an additional vehicle is being towed, or when members of your group commute to the park using a separate vehicle. (Such a vehicle must come from the registered party's address.
13. Do not take powerboats near swimmers; try not to disturb the tranquillity of those enjoying the beach.
14. Alcohol is allowed at your campsite. I had camped for years before I learned it was okay to consume a glass of wine with our dinner. Until then I had guiltily hid my drink from the park attendant I thought sure to expel me for my transgression. On one occasion, discovered and expecting to meet the full wrath of the BC Parks employee, I cowered and apologized. All he said was, "You can drink here. This is your home away from home. It is only in the public sections of the park that alcohol is prohibited." From that point on, I've always thought of provincial park camping spots as "home away from home."

Reservations

In 1996 BC Parks offered a new service which enabled advanced reservations to be made in 42 of the more popular provincial parks and in two national parks. During the first year of operation 36,857 reservations were made. If you do not have a reservation, campsites are available on a first come first served basis. Only a proportion of campsites in each campground are available for reservation. To make a reservation phone *Discover Camping Campground Reservation Service* 1-800-689-9025. In 1997 the fee to reserve was $6.00 per night to a maximum of $18.00 for three to 14 nights. Campers pay the reservation and campsite fees when making a reservation. Payment is taken from Mastercard or Visa and is subject to GST. Reservations are taken from 1 March to 15 September and sites can be reserved up to three months in advance, at least two days prior to arrival.

This service has proven immensely popular, although early would-be subscribers had long waits on the phone to make reservations. BC Parks now claim to have dealt with this issue and have implemented new software to help things run smoothly. As mentioned above, on arriving at a campground without a reservation, you should check the board at the gate for details on which spots are taken. While reservations offer the advantage of assuring accommodation for the night, the offset is that you have no choice over your spot and could be located next to a particularly well-used thunderbox (pit toilet) or at the busy entrance to the campground. For those who have found a full house at a popular campground on the times they have tried to visit, the reservation system provides a way to avoid uncertainty. (If reservations are accepted this information is conveyed under the "facilities" section describing the campground). Reservations are now accepted at Kootenay and Pacific Rim National Parks in addition to the following 44 provincial park campgrounds:

Alice Lake	Goldstream	Okanagan Lake
Bamberton	Gordon Bay	Otter Lake
Barkerville	Green Lake	Paarens Beach
Bear Creek	Haynes point	Porpoise Bay
Beatton	Herald	Porteau Cove
Beaumont	Kikomun Creek	Prior Centennial
Charlie Lake	Kokanee Creek	Rathtrevor
Champion Lakes	Lakelse Lake	Rolley Lake
Crooked River	Liard River Hotsprings	Saltery Bay
Cultus Lake	Manning	Sasquatch
Ellison	Miracle Beach	Shuswap lake
Englishman River Falls	Moberly Lake	Ten Mile Lake
Fintry	Montague Harbour	Tyhee
French Beach	Mount Robson	Wasa Lake
Golden Ears	Moyie Lake	

Potential Hazards

Information at the entrance to specific campgrounds lists hazards of the particular vicinity. Below is a synopsis of the more common problems and how to avoid them.

Swimmer's Itch

Parasites that live in freshwater snails and waterfowl can cause swimmer's itch or *cerarial dermatitis*, a temporary skin irritation. The larvae stage of the parasite invades human skin by mistake, and it cannot live in humans for long periods of time The larvae thrive close to the shore in warm waters of lakes and ponds where Canada Geese and other waterfowl are found. Because they go in and out of the water frequently and have tender skin, children are particularly at risk. Swimmer's itch can be avoided by applying skin oil (for example, baby oil) before swimming, towelling briskly, and showering after swimming. Swimmer's itch can be recognized by small red spots which can develop into small blisters. While unpleasant, the condition can be treated with calamine lotion and is usually self-eliminating within a week. As mentioned above, the information board at the entrance to the campground will show whether swimmer's itch is a problem at the lake you plan to visit.

Poison Ivy

This low, glossy plant with three green leaves and white berries can produce severe skin rashes. It is prevalent in sunny areas on Vancouver Island and in the Okanagan. Calamine lotion is an effective treatment.

Sunburn

You are living outdoors when camping and it is easy to forget how long you have been exposed to the sun. Always remember to apply and reapply sun screen, wear a hat, and be especially careful where water or snow can reflect the sun and compound the problem.

Water safety

Lifeguards are not employed in BC Parks, so a watchful eye must be kept on those who cannot swim. Some parks have designated swimming areas; others do not. Climatic conditions may change rapidly in some locations with winds suddenly developing and causing a hazard for boating enthusiasts. Again, information on the park's notice board will state whether this is a problem.

Bears

BC has almost one-quarter of all the black bears in Canada and about half the grizzlies. Although people-bear encounters are rare, campers should remember they are always in bear country in BC and should respect bears as strong, fast, wild animals and consequently act responsibly at all times.

BC Parks produces a leaflet entitled *Bears in Provincial Parks*. This brochure recommends the following precautions be taken in developed campgrounds to reduce and eliminate the odors that attract bears and to prevent bear attacks:

▲ Store food and garbage in airtight containers or in your vehicle, or suspend it at least 4 metres from the ground away from any tree trunk.

▲ Avoid fish smells as these strongly attract bears.

▲ Cook and eat away from your tent.

▲ Clean up immediately and do not leave cooking utensils, coolers, or dishwater around.

▲ Never bury garbage. Bears normally dig for food, and they may remember the location as a food source, thus endangering those visitors that follow.

▲ Avoid getting scents or food smells on clothing or sleeping bags.

▲ Women should consider using tampons if menstruating.

▲ Keep dogs on a leash.

▲ Always use a flashlight if walking at night.

Generally bears go out of their way to avoid people, but all bears are dangerous; they can rip apart tents and vehicles in search of food, run as fast as a race horse, have excellent sight and hearing and an acute sense of smell. They are strong swimmers, and black bears and young grizzlies are agile tree-climbers. Upon leaving the city you are in bear country and should use caution.

Anyone planning to camp or utilize the outdoors should learn how to recognize a black and grizzly bear and how to respond accordingly. Black bears can be black, brown, cinnamon, or blond with a straight face profile, short curved claws, and a small shoulder hump. Grizzly bears can also be black, brown, or blond, are bigger than black bears, have long curved claws, and a prominent shoulder hump. If walking in bear country watch for warning signs such as tracks, overturned rocks, clawed trees, chewed roots, and droppings. Talk loudly, wear bear bells, or sing to make your presence known. If you see a bear in the distance, leave the area immediately. If you encounter one at close range avoid eye contact, move away slowly, and stay calm. If the bear approaches standing up, it is trying to identify you. Talk quietly so it knows you are human. If it is lowering its head, flattening its ears, snapping its jaws, and snorting, the bear is displaying aggression. This is serious. Do not run but continue to back away. If a grizzly shows aggression, consider climbing a tree. Generally the key is to do nothing to threaten or arouse the animal. If a grizzly attacks, play dead and adopt a tight, curled-up position with your head on your knees and your hands behind your neck. Do not move until the bear leaves the area. If a black bear attacks, try to retreat from the attack. If an offensive attack takes place, for example when you are in your tent, try to retreat to a safe place and use weapons such as rocks and branches to deter the animal.

Never approach or feed bears. Food-conditioned bears—those that scavenge food from garbage cans and picnic tables—begin to associate food with people, loose their natural fear of humans, and become a threat to campers and to themselves. With caution and sensible behavior, you can safely camp in and enjoy bear country. (Further detailed information on bears can be found in a book by Gary Shelton entitled *Bear Encounter Survival Guide*).

What to Take Camping

To the uninitiated, it would appear that some people take everything camping. On one occasion I camped next to a couple who had a large RV with two mountain bikes tied to the front, a boat on the roof, and a small four-wheel-drive vehicle towed behind. Their picnic table displayed several coolers of assorted sizes, wine glasses, a bread basket, and a red checked tablecloth; overhead was an ornate striped awning. Artificial grass, potted plants, lanterns, and numerous plastic lounge chairs with cushions were strategically positioned around a huge barbecue. This campsite had more accoutrements than my home (and certainly was worth more). While it is impossible to provide the definitive list of necessities, there are a number of items which, if remembered, will make your camping experience more enjoyable whether you are a tenter or an "RVer."

▲ aluminum foil
▲ axe
▲ barbecue, hibachi
▲ biodegradable dish soap, scrubbing pads
▲ bungee cords
▲ camera and film
▲ candles/lantern
▲ first aid kit, including calamine lotion
▲ flashlight
▲ garbage bags
▲ insect repellent
▲ matches and newspaper for the campfire
▲ paper towels
▲ rainy day activities (books, Walkman, travel games)
▲ rope
▲ sunglasses, hat, and sun screen
▲ Swiss army knife
▲ tarp
▲ towels
▲ water container and funnel (to collect water from water pump)

I started my BC camping career in 1992 with a two-person tent (designed for two *very* small people) and toured the province in a 1974 Ford Pinto. On this first excursion I was totally unprepared. My partner and I had no axe, so to make a fire we had to arrive at a campground early enough to collect the unused wood that had been cut by our predecessors. On one occasion this option was not available so we approached a neighbouring site and asked a camper if we could borrow his axe. He came over from his well-equipped RV to supply the tool and chat. After surveying our meagre tent and picnic table (displaying two plastic plates, two plastic mugs, and one plastic Safeway bag of food), he started to explain how he started as we were doing, with barely the basics, but assured us that as each year progressed our commitment to camping would grow and more "comforts" would be acquired. He was right. While we have not progressed to the RV (yet) we now arrive at our campsite in a 1990s Mazda, sleep on self-inflating thermarests in a six-person tent you can stand up in, have tarps, a red checked tablecloth, clotheslines, coolers, a hibachi, and yes, even an axe. On occasion we see novice campers starting out as we and many other have done, and we look knowingly at each other, content in the thought that it will not be long before they too start to collect the camping necessities. One of the tremendous joys of camping is *learning* how to do it.

Camper Rentals

At least 26 RV rental companies detail their equipment offering and locations at the BC Ministry of Environment website: http://www.env.gov.bc.ca.

British Columbia Regions

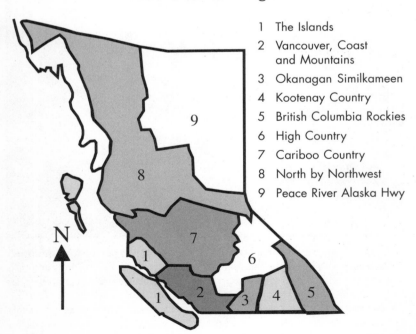

1. The Islands
2. Vancouver, Coast and Mountains
3. Okanagan Similkameen
4. Kootenay Country
5. British Columbia Rockies
6. High Country
7. Cariboo Country
8. North by Northwest
9. Peace River Alaska Hwy

1 The Islands

This chapter includes campgrounds located on Vancouver Island and the Gulf Islands. Vancouver Island is the largest North American island in the Pacific and stretches 450 kilometres. Named after Captain Vancouver, who discovered it in 1778, this varied region includes mountains, farmlands, miles of breathtaking coastline (lots of it inaccessible by road), and unique wildlife. The Gulf Islands are situated between Vancouver Island and the Mainland and for many residents offer a serene and alternative lifestyle away from the populations of the Lower Mainland and southern Vancouver Island. Tourists, too, find the islands a delight, and with 28 provincial park campgrounds available, accommodation should not be a problem.

Montague Harbour on Galiano Island.

Bamberton

Location
A true family-friendly campground and a really picturesque location, Bamberton looks on to the Finlayson Arm of the Saanich Inlet, across the Gulf Islands to Mount Baker, and beyond. Bamberton is situated about half an hour's drive from Victoria, one kilometre east of Highway 1 at Malahat Drive. Services are available on the Highway and in Victoria to the south and Duncan to the north.

Facilities
Nestled in a lightly forested area which includes arbutus trees (only found on Vancouver Island and the Lower Mainland) are 47 well-appointed, private camping

spots. There are flush and pit toilets but no sani-station nor showers. The park is accessible by wheelchairs and reserva-tions are accepted.

Recreational activities
This is a popular family recreational area as the warm waters of the Saanich Inlet together with over 225 metres of beach make it a pleasant place for families to congregate, play, and rest. Creeks that run through the park have little fishing potential, but it is possible to catch salmon in the Inlet. Small trails lead from the campground to the beach area, and interpretive programs are offered in the summer. As this provincial park is so close to Victoria, 30 minutes to the south, and Duncan, 20 minutes north, there are many additional things to see and do outside the immediate area. For example, just north of Duncan is a Forest Museum displaying logging artifacts and giving the history of an industry that is very much a part of Vancouver Island's heritage.

Additional information
Bamberton was given to the people of BC by the British Columbian Cement Company, and the name was chosen to commemorate H.K. Bamber, a former managing director of the company. Its proximity to Victoria and the population of southern Vancouver Island means Bamberton is a popular place for locals to spend weekends and therefore can become very busy. It is far more desirable than its nearest competitor, McDonald.

Elk Falls

Location.
This is a beautiful provincial park that features a cascading 25-metre waterfall created by the Campbell River falling into a walled canyon. In spring the waters tumble (and in late summer trickle) over a deep gorge and provide a beautiful vista. Elk Falls is located on Highway 28 just two kilometres north of Campbell River, where all services are available.

Facilities
Elk Falls boasts 122 large, private camping spots surrounded by trees; many of the more desirable spots are situated along the waters edge of the Quinsam River. There is a sani-station and a couple of flush toilets but no wheelchair accessibility.

Recreational activities
The primary attraction of the area is fishing, which in both Campbell River and Quinsam River is excellent. Depending on the time of year, steelhead, rainbow and cutthroat trout, and Dolly Varden can be caught. Another feature of this provincial park is the extensive trail system. The Quinsam River Trail leads to the Quinsam Salmon Hatchery while the Canyon View Trail takes explorers to the John Hart power-generating facility and an impressive bridge over the river. Other trails lead through woodland to wonderful waterfalls and wildlife viewing opportunities. For children there is

an adventure playground and sports field, and swimming and paddling is possible in the river at the day-use area. The nearby community of Campbell River is an attractive town to explore; look out for seals in the Georgia Strait.

Additional information
A magazine produced by BC Parks states: "The undisputedly cheapest overnight rate in the salmon capital of the world is located in Elk Falls Provincial Park. Just $9.50/ night (1997 prices) buys a quiet river setting, a campsite, a convenient location and a fishing extravaganza . . ." What more could you ask?

Salmon fishing is a favorite recreational activity. (courtesy Al Nickull)

Englishman River Falls

Location
Established in 1940, this 97-hectare provincial park is a delight to visit at any time of the year. Englishman River Falls is found 13 kilometres south of Parksville off Highway 4 on a paved road. Qualicum and Parksville are nearby.

Facilities
The campground has 105 spacious campsites set in a forest of Douglas-fir interspersed with Rocky Mountain maple trees and ferns. There are no showers, flush toilets, or sani-station, and only the basic camping facilities exist (pit toilets, wood, water, picnic tables, fire pit). The park is not wheelchair accessible. Reservations are accepted.

Recreational activities
In this park you can walk and take hiking trails to the beautiful waterfalls, among a mixed forest of cedar, fir, and hemlock; swim in the scenic river's

swimming holes; and fish. A deep pool at the bottom of the canyon is a good place to view spawning salmon, steelhead, and trout. The park's proximity to Nanaimo, Courtenay, and Port Alberni means the activities and facilities of these communities are easily accessible, as indeed is the beach at Parksville, where at low tide the sea recedes nearly 100 metres and leaves a vast expanse of sand and pools to explore and beachcomb.

Additional information
Originally named "Rio De Grullas" — River of Cranes — by the Spanish explorers of the eighteenth century, this river was renamed a century later in memory of an English immigrant who died here. The campground is frequently utilized when the one at Rathtrevor Beach is full. It is well worth visiting in the fall when the trees are turning beautiful shades of golden and red, or in the spring when the wildflowers are at their best.

(courtesy Al Nickull)

20

Fillongley

Location
There is something for everyone in this 23-hectare provincial park which includes a beach, a marshy estuary, a forest rich in old-growth firs, and the remnants of what was once a large estate. Found on the eastern side of Denman Island and featuring views of Lambert Channel, Fillongley is reached by ferry from Courtenay to Denman and then by taking a four-kilometre paved road to the east coast of the island where the campground is situated. Denman Island has food, gas, and basic supplies.

Facilities
The biggest drawback of Denman Island's only provincial park is that there are only ten camping spots available here and these spots are lined up side by side at the parking area. For more privacy it is possible to pitch tents under nearby trees. All basic amenities are provided (wood, water, pit toilets, picnic tables, fire pit).

Recreational activities
The campground is situated near a lovely rocky beach from which it is possible to swim, beachcomb, and look for oysters and clams. Hiking trails through old-growth forest have also been developed and offer an alternative to the shoreline recreational pursuits. The island is ideal for cycling enthusiasts as there is little traffic (except near the ferry terminals) and it is relatively flat. Denman Island is a delightful place to explore, for it has a beautifully relaxed atmosphere and many arts and crafts shops. In addition, nearby Hornby Island, which is also easy to reach, has hiking trails and lovely beaches.

Additional information
The park was bequeathed to the Province by George Beadnell, who named it after his home in England. Beadnell, one of the first pioneers to come to the area, built up the estate, which at its peak had a tennis court, bowling green, clubhouse, and greenhouse as well as a large, impressive home. Following his death in 1958, these facilities fell into disrepair and were eventually destroyed. Beadnell is buried in the park.

French Beach

Location
French Beach Provincial Park, which boasts over 1,600 metres of beach and exceptional views across the Strait of Juan de Fuca towards the Olympic Mountains in Washington State, is a marvellous place to visit. The 59-hectare park is located just 20 kilometres west of Sooke on Highway 14 (34 kilometres from Victoria). Services are therefore within easy reach.

Facilities
Set in a forest of Douglas-fir, Sitka spruce, western hemlock, and western redcedar are 69 shaded camping spots. There is a sani-station but only pit toilets. The park is wheelchair accessible and reservations are accepted.

Recreational activities
One of the biggest attractions here is whale watching. Magnificent grey whales migrate to their feeding grounds in the spring and return in the fall. If you're lucky, you can view them from the beach, or, if you are an experienced paddler, at closer range in a kayak. Roaming pods of killer whales are also sometimes observed. In looking offshore it is not unusual to see river otters, seals, and sea lions playing, while ospreys and bald eagles frequent the skies overhead. The extensive sand and gravel beach rimmed by the forest is a beautiful place to swim from. Small nature trails exist in the second-growth forest and there is a play park for children. Once you have had enough of the natural beauty, go and explore Victoria's many attractions.

Additional information
The biggest draw to this provincial park is the huge beach, a beautiful place to sit and watch the sun go down and to star-gaze. This is a perfect location to kick back and open Garnet Basque's *Lost Bonanzas of Western Canada*. Why? Because not far away, on the Leetch River, was the site of Vancouver Island's first gold rush. With another Basque book, *Gold Panner's Manual,* and a twenty-dollar gold pan, who knows, you might strike it rich.

Travel north to visit this lovely San Juan beach. (courtesy Garnet Basque)

Goldstream

Location

The BC Parks information leaflet for Goldstream reads: "Massive tress, majestic waterfalls, a meandering river that meets the sea, flowers, birds and fascinating fish are but a few attractions that draw people to Goldstream Provincial Park." This description, coupled with the fact that the park is only 19 kilometres northwest of Victoria off Highway 1, makes it a popular location for both locals and tourists.

Facilities

The park has 159 well-appointed camping spots available for every type of recreational vehicle. There are showers, a sani-station, flush and pit toilets, and wheelchair accessibility. Reservations are accepted.

Recreational activities

Goldstream is blessed with a number of hiking and walking routes, some accessible to mountain bikers. Trails take hikers through Goldstream's two distinctive vegetation zones to views of 600-year-old Douglas-fir trees and many other deciduous and evergreen trees and plants. The Gold Mine and Lower Falls Trail lead to Niagara Falls, which is higher than its namesake (and fortunately much less commercialized—no honeymoon suites here). Swimming and fishing are possible within the park, and in the summer months naturalists conduct interpretive programs in the outdoor theatre. A visitor centre is also located here.

Additional information

Goldstream River was first named Gold Creek in 1858 by Lieutenant Peter Leech, an engineer with the Vancouver Island Exploration Committee, who discovered gold in the waters. Subsequent exploration revealed only small deposits, but there is nothing stopping the fortune-seeker from further exploration . . . The Goldstream River is now the site of chum salmon spawning, and from mid-October to November draws many thousands of visitors and millions of salmon. BC Parks produces a leaflet detailing the salmon spawning process. Long ago, this area, like many others on Vancouver Island, was used by the native Coast Salish people as a fishing ground. Whether you are a fortune-seeker, an angler, or just a holiday-maker, Goldstream is a lovely place to choose to stop.

Welcome to Goldstream Provincial Park.
Enjoy Your Stay!

Gordon Bay

Location

Make sure you have the sun screen if you plan to holiday in one of Canada's hottest spots; Gordon Bay Provincial Park. This 49-hectare park is found at the southern section of Lake Cowichan, 35 kilometres west of Duncan. It can be accessed by taking Highway 18 just north of Duncan. The nearby community of Lake Cowichan has most services.

Facilities

Positioned in an area of second growth Douglas-fir, this campground has 130 large, well-structured camping spots (those numbered 1 to 14 being closest to the bay). There are flush and pit toilets, a sani-station, showers, and full access for the disabled. Reservations are accepted.

Recreational activities

Gordon Bay is located in one of the warmest valleys on Vancouver Island. The mountains pressing closely to Cowichan Lake produce a heat trap that ensures the highest average daily temperature in Canada. In the summer this means 24 degrees Celsius. The waters of Lake Cowichan supply relief from this heat (as do the shady camping spots). For the angler, the lake has reserves of Dolly Varden, rainbow and cutthroat trout, chum, coho, and spring salmon. There is a boat launch in the park and water skiing is permitted. An adventure playground has been constructed for children within the camping area and during the summer interpretive programs take place. Trails lead from the park over a forest floor covered with thimbleberry, salal, salmonberry, and, in the spring, wonderful wildflowers. (Remember, picking the vegetation in BC Parks is prohibited).

Additional information

In addition to the beauty of the park itself, the immediate surrounding area provides alternative activities. A small museum at Saywell Park offers local interest, and in Lake Cowichan, tours of the Earth Satellite Station are given.

In summary, Gordon Bay is a delightful family-oriented camping location equipped with all amenities. But be warned, as one of the most popular campgrounds on South Vancouver Island, it is frequently full.

Ironically, this remote community is the breeding ground of Canada's premier female golfer of the past decade. Dawn Coe-Jones, a repeat winner on the PGA tour, learned her golf here at March Meadows, the attractive nine-hole course in Honeymoon Bay that is open to the public.

Little Qualicum Falls

Location

This 444-hectare provincial park, claimed by some to be the most magnificent park on Vancouver Island, is characterized by impressive waterfalls that cascade into a rocky gorge. Little Qualicum River drops several hundred feet down the slopes of Mount Arrowsmith in a series of waterfalls. This remarkable vista is located on Highway 4, 19 kilometres west of Parksville on Little Qualicum River. Services are available at Port Alberni and Parksville.

Little Qualicum Falls.
(courtesy Al Nickull)

Facilities

Ninety-one camping spots are here for the taking in a pleasant pine forest setting. The park is accessible for the disabled, and there are flush and pit toilets but no showers or sanistation. The campground is quite near to the road and railway line.

Recreational activities

Swimming in this provincial park is wonderful and can be undertaken either in lovely little green pools within the river itself, or at the Beaufort and Cameron Lake picnic sites. There are over six kilometres of graded walking trails and fishing in the river is rewarding. Just outside the park is MacMillan (Cathedral Grove) Provincial Park, where magnificent western hemlock, Douglas-fir, and western redcedar stand over 200 feet tall, like the columns of a cathedral. Some of these trees are over 800 years old. Cathedral Grove has trails which lead into the depths of the spectacular old-growth forest.

Additional information

The area around the Beaufort and Cameron Lakes contains salamanders and newts which like the cool, damp cedar and fir forest area. This provincial park is conveniently located to explore the eastern Parksville/Qualicum area and the western town of Port Alberni. From Port Alberni it is possible to take the famous MV *Lady Rose* through the fjord scenery of the Alberni Inlet to Bamfield on the west coast, an unusual and rewarding trip which starts at 8:00 a.m. and returns around 6:00 p.m. If it is not raining, you will be guaranteed to see some spectacular scenery and unusual wildlife.

McDonald

Location

If you have missed the last ferry to the mainland you will be thankful for this provincial park at the end of the Saanich Peninsula. McDonald Provincial Park has good views of the nearby islands and is geared to overnight stays. Located two kilometres from the ferry terminal north of Sidney, the park primarily provides accommodation for travellers waiting to take the ferry from Swartz Bay.

Facilities

Fifty-one functional camping spots are available here for vehicles, along with an additional seven walk-in spots. Despite being near to considerable development, McDonald Provincial Park has only the basic facilities (wood, fire pit, picnic tables, pit toilets, water), but it does have access for the disabled.

Recreational activities

As mentioned above, McDonald Provincial Park is primarily used by those waiting to catch a ferry, or by those who have just taken a ferry and are therefore only staying one night. The park therefore offers little in the way of recreational pursuits. The town of Sidney, which has a pleasant harbour, craft shops, and cafes, is within easy access and can be explored. In the summer a small passenger ferry can be taken to Sidney Island, which has delightful scenery and a provincial park.

Additional information

Victoria, only a thirty-minute drive from Swartz Bay, offers a host of cultural and recreational activities for those who find they have time on their hands. Victoria is the capital of British Columbia and houses the legislature. Along streets lined with trees and flowers the fascinating British Columbia Museum, Empress Hotel, Parliament Buildings, Inner Harbour, and Chinatown are all within easy walking distance of one another. Shopping here is also a real treat. For those who have a choice and a vehicle, Bamberton Provincial Park is preferable to McDonald, but for those who are tired after a long day's travelling and just want a place for the night, McDonald delivers the goods.

Ferry Schedules

Current BC Ferry schedules are always available at BC Tourism centres and in most hotels. Worldwide, ferry information may be found at the BC Ferries web site http://www.bcferries.bc.ca.

Miracle Beach

Location

Blessed with excellent views across the Georgia Strait to the mainland mountains and a wide sandy beach, this campground is attractive to both adults and children, thus providing an ideal spot for a family vacation. Miracle Beach is located on the protected shores of the east coast of Vancouver Island, midway between Courtenay and Campbell River, 1½ kilometres from Highway 19 on a paved access road. The campground has all required services conveniently located on the highway and in nearby communities.

Facilities

Miracle Beach boasts 193 large, private camping spots in second-growth forest of Douglas-fir, hemlock, and western redcedar. All amenities are here including showers, flush and pit toilets, a sani-station, and access for the disabled. Reservations are accepted.

Recreational activities

One of the main attractions is the lovely long sandy beach, perfect for swimming, sunbathing, and exploring tide pools when they are accessible. To supplement personal investigations, the excellent Visitor Centre has saltwater aquariums, nature displays, and interpretive programs. Black Creek, which runs through the park, has a coho salmon run, and there are two small walking trails. For those who choose to travel farther afield, the salmon fishing in the area is good, and short boat trips can be taken to the nearby islands of Denman, Hornby, Quadra, and Cortes. At night, clear skies make for excellent star-gazing opportunities from the beach or your camping spot.

Additional information

Miracle Beach is said to have received its name because it was miraculously missed by two severe forest fires that devastated much of the surrounding forest area in the recent past. When I stayed here, children seemed to outnumber adults ten to one, and a quiet sunbathe for a single woman was an elusive dream. This provincial park is an extremely popular camping location, especially during the summer months. In 1995, over 16,000 camping parties registered at this delightful family vacation spot.

Montague Harbour

Location

When Montague Harbour Provincial Marine Park on Galiano Island opened in 1959, it was the first provincial park to serve visitors who arrived in their own boats as well as those who came by car or on foot. The park encompasses an 89-hectare area which starts five metres below sea level and increases to 180 metres above. Galiano Island can be reached via BC Ferries, either from Swartz Bay on Vancouver Island or Tsawwassen on the mainland. From the ferry dock at Sturdies Bay on Galiano, you must drive ten kilometres to the park. Full services are at Sturdies Bay, and the marina has a small store and coffee bar with basic supplies.

Facilities

There are 40 beautifully positioned camping spots here, 25 of them suitable for vehicles and set in a forested area. Many of the 15 walk-in sites overlook the harbour and therefore have better views than the drive-in spots. Facilities are restricted to the basic ones found in BC Parks (pit toilets, wood, water, picnic tables, fire pit); there is no sani-station nor access for the disabled. Reservations are accepted.

Recreational activities

This gorgeous park has scenic hiking trails which lead through a forested area of arbutus, Douglas-fir, hemlock, and Garry oak to beautiful sandy beaches of white sand and shell, ideal for sunbathing or swimming from. The abundant salmon and shellfish in the area attract a wide array of birds, including bald eagles, which can easily be seen fishing for their dinner. Canoes and kayaks can be hired from the adjacent marina and there is a boat launch within the park. Galiano Island has quite a unique feel about it. Many artists and crafts people have chosen to live here, and the area around Sturdies Bay has a small number of restaurants, craft shops, and an excellent bakery.

Additional information

On weekends in the summer months, the island's only neighbourhood pub offers a free hourly bus service between itself and the marina (adjacent to the campground). The pub has live music and good food, while the marina serves excellent cinnamon buns and coffee in the morning. The island is named after the Spanish explorer Captain Galiano, who discovered the Gulf Islands in 1792. Another provincial park on Galiano, Dionisio Point, is on the northern tip of the island and has limited camping facilities (no water or wood and only walk-in camping) but a lovely beach area to explore. Smaller and less commercialized than Salt Spring Island but with more amenities than Pender, Galiano is a fantastic place to spend some time. The sunsets from the campground are astoundingly beautiful.

Morton Lake

Location
A really serene camping experience can be had at this exquisite little park that nestles in the Sayward Forest northwest of Campbell River on both the Mohun and Morton Lakes. The park is reached by travelling on Highway 19 for 27 kilometres north of Campbell River and then by taking Menzies Bay logging road (gravel) for 20 kilometres. Services are at Campbell River, 47 kilometres to the south.

Facilities
There are only 24 camping spots here, but many of them have access directly on to Morton Lake and are quite charming. Only the basic amenities are available (pit toilets, wood, water, fire pit, picnic tables).

Recreational activities
Visitors to this area can enjoy fishing, boating, swimming and canoeing in either Mohun or Morton Lakes. Alternatively, a trail leads to Andrew Lake and provides a different venue for water-based recreational pursuits. There is a good sandy beach by the campground, and as this location is away from the nearest centre of population, sunbathing and swimming can be a tranquil experience.

Additional information
The forest around the lake was destroyed in the Great Campbell River Fire of 1938 and has subsequently been replaced by Douglas-fir, while pine, cedar, and hemlock have all grown back naturally. The scars of the fire are still clearly evident in the area. Unfortunately, this is the most northern provincial park on Vancouver Island that has the basic camping amenities. Although there are two others, Marble River and Schoen Lake, neither has fresh water or firewood, and when I tried to stay at Schoen Lake in September 1995 it was closed. In contrast to the roads south of Campbell River, Highway 19 north is very quiet and a beautiful drive; it is a great pity that there are not provincial parks located along this stretch of highway. In all my years of camping it is only in the northern part of Vancouver Island that I have out of necessity stayed in a private campground. Although in comparison to other provinces, states, and countries BC may have a large number of provincial parks, there is still a need for more, especially on northern Vancouver Island.

If you are driving northward stop at Telegraph Cove for a visit.
(courtesy The BC Adventure Network)

Newcastle Island

Location

A small island barely a kilometre from Nanaimo, with spectacular views across to the mainland mountains, Newcastle can only be reached by water. Newcastle Island Provincial Marine Park is a popular cruising destination for recreational boaters. From Nanaimo, a charming little paddle steamer operates from Maffeo Sutton Park behind the civic arena to ferry foot passengers to the island. Services are available in Nanaimo, although food can be purchased in the tea rooms located in the pavilion on the island.

Facilities

There are only 18 designated camping spots, beautifully positioned at the edge of the forest, but a vast grassland meadow accommodates all additional campers. Many prefer this open space as it is closer to the water. There are flush and pit toilets and the park is wheelchair accessible.

Recreational activities

The island is rich in history; the Coast Salish People inhabited the area for centuries prior to the Spanish exploration in 1791. With the help of the indigenous people the Hudson's Bay Company opened a coal mine on the island and named it Newcastle after the famous British mining town. Coal was extracted until 1887. From 1869 until 1955 a sandstone quarry was in operation. Evidence of the past can be seen when you take the hiking trails that zigzag their way around and across the park. Bikes are permitted on two of these trails. There are a number of beaches, caves, and bays to explore and a calm sea to swim in. Canoeing around the shoreline is a favourite pastime and there is a children's play area. Deer can be seen grazing in the early evening, and the area is also noted for its shoreline bird life.

Additional information

In July 1995 and 1996 the Cappa Big Band has played in Newcastle Island Pavilion. On each of these occasions we left Vancouver with rucksacks on our backs, caught two buses to the ferry at Horseshoe Bay ($1.50), the ferry from Horseshoe Bay to Nanaimo ($6.50) and walked the thirty-minute route from the ferry terminal to the paddle steamer to go and camp on the island, hike the trails during the day, eat on the verandah of the licensed tea rooms during the evening, then dance the night away to the sound of brilliant jazz music. On both these occasions I think we were the only couple wearing shorts, but we had such fun for only $17.00 (price includes the ferry ride from Nanaimo, normally $4.00 return). It is delightful to round off a perfect day with a glass of whisky, good music still ringing in your ears, and to know that your bed is just a short walk away across starlit fields.

Note: Mid-Vancouver Island campers will find a good hiking guide in Fred Rogers' *Southern Vancouver Island Hiking Trails* (Heritage House).

Pacific Rim National

Location
Pacific Rim National Park boasts an 11-kilometre-long stretch of pristine surf-swept shoreline. Three distinctively different locations make up this 51,300-hectare (including 22,300 hectares of ocean) national park, and in order to see all aspects you need at least two weeks. The park's features include the famous West Coast Trail, a 77-kilometre rugged excursion into west coast rain forest scenery, (reservations are required if you intend to take this hike); the Broken Islands—a group of over 100 islands in Barkley Sound; and Long Beach, with it's fantastic sands. Pacific Rim is on the west coast of Vancouver Island on Highway 4. Services are available at Ucluelet, Tofino, and along the highway between these two settlements.

Facilities
Developed vehicle-accessible camping facilities are available at the Long Beach area of the park (wilderness camping is possible in other areas). The main vehicle/tent campground is Green Point with 94 blissful spots located high above the beach. Here campers are lulled to sleep by the sound of the ocean and facilities include a sani-station, flush and pit toilets, a visitor centre and limited access for the disabled. During the summer months this campground is almost always full. A smaller, more primitive campground named Schooner Cove has walk-in camping for 80 tents and requires a 15-minute trek from the parking lot. It has water and pit toilets, and wood can be collected from the beach to make fires. Reservations are accepted at Green Point, and as Pacific Rim is a national park, a fee is charged for firewood.

Recreational activities
Long Beach provides a superb expanse of shoreline for surfers, windsurfers, swimmers, and kayakers to demonstrate their skills. As the wild waves of the Pacific Ocean pound along the sands, beachcombing and hiking are invigorating activities here in any season, as long as you have the correct attire. The temperature of the ocean varies from six to twelve degrees centigrade, bald eagles frequent the area, and there are eight small (one- to two-kilometre) trails that can be walked to explore the rain forest or coastal flora and fauna. The community of Tofino is rapidly developing into a tourist facility and offers commercial services including excursions in the area.

Long Beach is a great place for a stroll.
(courtesy Al Nickull)

Additional information

The Canadian Park Service has produced a number of leaflets about Pacific Rim, including one that lists the hiking trails. These can be obtained from the information centre. Long Beach is extremely popular in the peak summer months but offers just as many delights for those who choose to avoid the crowds and visit at cooler times. Be warned that precipitation is common; the region receives 300 centimetres of rain a year, so if you are visiting out of season, dress accordingly. If you do manage to camp in one of the two campgrounds you may well wake to find the previous evening's ocean view obscured by a heavy morning mist. During the course of the day the mist usually evaporates, leaving you again to enjoy the sight as well as the sound of the ocean.

(Top) Beachcoming, treasures to find at Long Beach.
(Bottom) A mother bear and her twin cubs at Long Beach.
(courtesy Al Nickull)

Prior Centennial

Location

For a "get-away-from-it-all" camping experience you cannot go far wrong in selecting Prior Centennial, North Pender Island's only provincial park. Ferries to the Island can be taken from Tsawwassen on the mainland or Swartz Bay on Vancouver Island. The campground is located 6 kilometres from the ferry terminal on Canal Road. Stores exist in Port Washington, Hope Bay, and Port Browning .

Facilities

This is a relatively small, 16-hectare provincial park nestled in a pleasant forested area. Seventeen well-spaced vehicle/tent sites exist. All basic services can be found here (wood, water, fire pit, pit toilet, picnic tables). Reservations are accepted.

Recreational activities

The campground's location a few hundred metres from Medicine Beach on Bedwell Harbour is ideal for beachcombing and shoreline explorations. Hiking trails exist and Pender Island is great to explore by bike. Look out for the historical markers which give details of the island's past. The small settlement of Hope Bay—with the oldest building on the island, the 1912 Hope Bay Heritage Store, as well as a couple of galleries and coffee shops—is a pleasant place to relax and watch the world go by.

Additional information

This park was donated to BC Parks in 1958 by Mr. and Mrs. F.L. Prior, hence it's name. Pender Island is one of the Gulf Islands and only a short ferry ride from Galiano Island and Salt Spring Island, which both have provincial parks. Many tourists vacation by "island hopping" between these relaxed locations, while residents of the Lower Mainland and Vancouver Island visit to enjoy the all-together-different ambiance created by the island lifestyle. Access to South Pender Island is from a wooden bridge one kilometre from the campground, and while there is more to explore on North Pender Island, it is interesting to travel south as the ambiance of the island changes.

Picnic at a shelter in some provincial campsites.
(courtesy Al Nickull)

Rathtrevor Beach

Location

Cool ocean waters lapping a long white beach are just one of the many attractions of Rathtrevor Beach Provincial Park. Situated on Highway 19 two kilometres south of Parksville, with views on to the Georgia Strait and the Coast mountains

(courtesy BC Parks)

beyond, Rathtrevor Beach regularly sees over 160,000 visitors per year. It is the most popular park on Vancouver Island in which to camp. Services are available in Parksville.

Facilities

The 175 camping spots are located in the Douglas-fir forested area of the park and accommodate every type of recreational vehicle. The campground is fully equipped with a sani-station, showers, flush and pit toilets, and wheelchair accessibility. Reservations are accepted.

Recreational activities

Famed for its beautiful sandy shingle on 2,000 metres of beach leading to warm, clear waters, Rathtrevor Beach is described in BC Parks literature as "unbeatable for swimming." Windsurfing and canoeing is possible (there is no boat launch), and a number of walks and self-guided nature trails exist. Bird-watching is reputed to be good in the springtime and during the annual herring spawn. There are two children's play areas and in the summer months the amphitheatre is used to deliver visitors' programs. Each year the park hosts "Rath Farm Days" to celebrate the park's former life as a farm. The old farmhouse is now the park visitor centre.

Additional information

Rathtrevor received its name from a gold prospector and pioneer, William Rath, who settled in the area with his wife and family in 1886. In 1903 he died, leaving his wife with the farm and five children. She eventually developed the land into a campground and added the word "trevor" for effect. Rathtrevor was acquired by BC Parks in 1967. Today this campground is extremely popular. Visitors who arrive to find it full do not, however, have far to travel to find alternative provincial park camping as Englishman River Falls Provincial Park is only 13 kilometres away, and Little Qualicum Falls is 24 kilometres from Rathtrevor.

Ruckle

Location

In 1974 the Ruckle family sold a 486-hectare area of land to the provincial government for a nominal fee. In so doing they gave the people of BC and visitors to the province a superb location in which to camp. The park is situated 12 kilometres from Fulford Harbour at Beaver Point at the southeastern corner of Salt Spring Island (locals prefer Saltspring Island). It is the largest park in the Gulf Islands. The nearest services can be found at Fulford Harbour.

(courtesy BC Parks)

Facilities

The park contains 70 walk-in camping spots in a grassy area beside Swanson Channel. There is parking for RVs but no campsites immediately adjacent. The walk from the parking area to the campground is flat and in under five minutes you can pitch your tent on a site looking directly over the water. All the basic amenities are found here (pit toilets, wood, water, picnic tables, fire pit). There is no sani-station or access for the disabled.

Recreational activities

From the position of the tent, campers can observe otters, harbour seals, porpoise, sea lions—and if very fortunate—killer whales as they swim in the adjacent waters. Ruckle Park has over seven kilometres of shoreline characterized by pocket beaches, rocky coves, and headlands waiting to be explored. A number of walking trails in the park lead around the headlands and through the forested areas. Swimming, beachcombing, and scuba diving are all possible here, while a maze of paved roads make cycling a delight.

Additional information

The park was originally settled in 1872 by the Ruckle family, who still reside and work in the area. The continuous use of the land for farming purposes from the late 1800s until today makes it one of BC's oldest family farms. The Ruckle family retain their right to life tenancy within the park, while visitors can tour the historical farm buildings and learn of farming practices of a bygone age. Descriptive markers and photographs attached to the well-maintained historical buildings give details of a past life. Ruckle is another superb location to stay and enjoy British Columbia.

Sidney Spit Marine

Location

Although effectively a marine park, this lovely camping facility deserves mentioning. Sidney Spit Provincial Marine Park is on Sidney Island and has no vehicle access. It can be reached by taking a foot passenger ferry which departs from Government Wharf at the end of Beacon Avenue in Sidney on Vancouver Island. Services are found in Sidney.

Facilities

The park has 20 formal walk-in camping spots in addition to group camping facilities and plenty of space for spillover camping. All the basic amenities are provided (pit toilets, wood, water, fire pit, picnic tables).

Recreational activities

BC Parks literature describes Sidney Spit as ". . . one of the most beautiful marine parks in the Pacific Northwest" as it features thousands of metres of white sandy beach backed by towering bluffs. Beyond these the uplands contain a second-growth forest of fir, maple, western redcedar, and arbutus. One of it's main features is a lagoon awarding one of the best opportunities to explore intertidal life. These salt marshes and tidal flats attract both human and animal forms: ornithologists, naturalists, seals, orcas, and dolphins are all occasionally seen. Trails lead around the park while the stunning beach provides opportunities to swim, sunbathe, fish, and boat.

Additional information

Some of the bricks used to build the famous Empress Hotel in Victoria and the Hotel Vancouver in Vancouver were taken from a brick factory which operated at the turn of the century at the southern wharf of Sidney Island. At its peak this factory employed 70 workers. In 1924 the Todd family began purchasing land on Sidney and by 1968 owned all but one-tenth, which had been acquired by the government in 1924. This is the tenth (400 hectares) which we thankfully all have access to today. The community of Sidney is an enjoyable place for an afternoon stroll; in addition to shops that sell arts, crafts, and antiques, there are inviting delis and cafes that offer an assortment of refreshments to revitalize a tired camper.

Feel free to leave your "home" while you explore the area.

Smelt Bay

Location
Located on the southern peninsula of Cortes Island with stunning views to the south and west across a long pebble beach, Smelt Bay is the only provincial park on the island that permits camping. Cortes Island is not easy to reach but is well worth the effort. You must take two ferries, the first from Campbell River to Quadra Island and the second from Quadra on to Cortes. A 25-kilometre paved road leads from the ferry to the campground. Services are available on the island at Whitecove, Mansons Landing, and Squirrel Cove.

Facilities
Twenty-two camping spots are available in the woods set back from the beach with, as one would expect, only the basic facilities being supplied (water, wood, pit toilets, picnic tables, fire pit).

Recreational activities
Leisure pursuits in the area include beachcombing, swimming, fishing, and generally relaxing. At low tide the pebble beach which leads to Sutil Point reveals a fascinating array of rock pools waiting to be explored. (Sutil Point is named after the Spanish ship *Sutil* in which Captain Galiano explored these waters in 1792). The immediate area of the park is rich in history, for example, the mounds behind the gravel beach having been built centuries ago by the Salish people for defense purposes against the Yacultas. Cycling around the Island is a pleasant, easy activity as the traffic is minimal and the roads paved. Cortes is a quiet, remote island very different from Quadra; Cortes has few settlements and a unique charm. Most of the development is concentrated in the south.

Additional information
Smelt Bay was created in 1973 to offer camping facilities and to protect an indigenous cultural site. The park is named after the smelt fish which at certain times of the year spawn by the tens of thousands in this vicinity. A lovely quiet getaway spot, Cortes Island is one of the more scenic islands and has an intricate coastline ideal for canoeing and kayaking.

Sproat Lake

Location
Situated on the northern shore of Sproat Lake 13 kilometres from Port Alberni off Highway 4 is the popular family campground of Sprout Lake. There is something for everyone. Campers who stay here can marvel at both the natural beauty of the area and the display of aviation technology.

Facilities
Excellent camping can be had at Sproat Lake. The campground is situated in a forested area near the river and has showers, flush and pit toilets, and a sani-station available for tenants of the 59 spots. There are two campgrounds straggling the highway, the more desirable one being nearer the lake. The park is wheelchair accessible. Reservations are not accepted.

Recreational activities
Sproat Lake is noted for it's warm waters, fantastic for swimming. There is a large boat launch and good fishing. Trails lead through the forested area of second-growth Douglas-fir, where at certain times of the year the ground is littered with an attractive assortment of wildflowers. The prehistoric pictographs found along trails at the southern end of the park are testimony to man's presence in the area over the centuries. In addition, the nearby town of Port Alberni is a pleasant community to explore.

Additional information
During the summer visitors can see huge Martin Mars bombing planes take off from their lakeside base to extinguish fires. These, the world's largest water bombers, are operated by a collective of five BC forest companies. The planes can load 32 tons of water within 22 seconds by skimming across the lake at over 110 kilometres per hour. The economy of Vancouver Island is dependent on the logging industry, and the threat of fires here, and in the rest of BC, peaks during the summer camping season. It is therefore imperative all campfires are extinguished properly before a campsite is vacated. If the threat of fire becomes too great, fires are forbidden in provincial parks, and information leaflets are posted to inform campers.

Mars Martin water bomber arriving at Sproat Lake. (courtesy Grant Wood)

Stamp Falls

Location

An angler's delight, this park is extremely popular with fishermen who visit the area for the excellent steelhead, coho, and cutthroat trout that can be caught. Located 14 kilometres north of Port Alberni off Highway 4 on a paved road, Stamp Falls has a lovely rural setting and yet is close to all amenities at Port Alberni.

Facilities

There are 22 camping spots available here, some pleasantly located in a forested area near the river. Only the basic facilities exist (water, wood, pit toilets, picnic tables, fire pit).

Recreational activities

If you enjoy fishing you'll love Stamp Falls as the main attraction here is the fish. The campground often is used as a base camp for anglers who wish to explore the lakes and rivers in the vicinity. The unique feature of the park is the fascinating display of salmon ascending the fish ladders in the summer and early fall. In July and August 30,000 sockeye salmon use this route, with lesser numbers of Chinook and coho following in September and October. Trails lead visitors from the campground to the fish ladders and to the views of the waterfalls in Stamp River.

Additional information

This 236-hectare park was created in 1940 and is named after an early pioneer who built Alberni's first sawmill. The location makes a pleasant and interesting picnic spot for travellers heading along Route 4. Stamp Falls is the closest provincial park (with camping facilities) to Pacific Rim National Park approximately 100 kilometres to the west. The highway between Port Alberni and Tofino is quite beautiful and follows the clear, tumbling waters of the Kennedy River for half of its route. Upon reaching Pacific Rim National Park near Tofino, the traveller is rewarded with dramatic views of the Pacific.

Try your hand at fishing, maybe you'll be lucky too! (courtesy Dennis Hurd)

Strathcona

Location

Established in 1911, Strathcona is BC's oldest provincial park and is located in a majestic wilderness of old-growth forest, mountain peaks, clear rivers, waterfalls, and lakes encompassing more than 210,000 hectares. The main route to the park is from Campbell River on Highway 28, which runs through the park and connects to Gold River on the west of the Island. All services are available in Campbell River, and there is a private lodge in the park that has food, accommodation, and canoe/kayak rentals. Fuel is not available in the park.

Facilities

In addition to wilderness camping, the primary camping spots are in two locations on Buttle Lake. Buttle Lake campground has 85 units and Ralph River has 76. Facilities at both these locations include pit toilets, wood, water, fire pit, and picnic tables. There is no sani-station nor access for the disabled.

Recreational activities

As would be expected, there is a great deal to see and do in Strathcona Park, and it is easy to spend a week here. From Buttle Lake there are 12 hiking and walking trails that take explorers on a variety of hikes; in addition there are a number of shorter nature trails. Other areas of the park also have developed trail systems, details of which can be obtained from a leaflet produced by BC Parks. Swimming in Buttle Lake is good from both the campgrounds, and there are two boat launches. Water-skiing is permitted on the lake and, as mentioned above, the nearby lodge rents canoes and kayaks. A wealth of streams, rivers, and lakes provide angling opportunities. There are excellent wildlife viewing opportunities as well. The southern section of the park contains Della Falls, Canada's highest waterfall at 440 metres, and the tenth highest in the world. With the spring runoff in the months of May and June, the falls are particularly spectacular

Additional information

Strathcona is named after Donald Alexander Smith, First Baron Strathcona and Mount Royal, who was a Canadian pioneer and one of the principals involved with the construction of the Canadian Pacific Railway. Interestingly, the wildlife populations in the park (and on Vancouver Island) differ from those of the mainland, as chipmunks, rabbits, coyotes, foxes, and moose are not found here. Strathcona is an excellent location for those who enjoy hiking and the outdoor life and definitely justifies more than a one-night stay. The road from Campbell River to Gold River traverses much of the park and is a pleasant, quiet drive.

Additional Campgrounds

Beaumont Marine

Beaumont Marine Provincial Park on the west side of South Pender Island is accessible only by boat. It has 11 walk-in camping spots, four pit toilets, and fresh water (no wood). The area is noted for unique sandstone formations along the beach and is close to Bedwell Harbour Village, which has a store, post office, and fuel. A series of trails are available, and the coast supplies swimming, beachcombing, fishing, and canoeing possibilities.

Cowichan River

Found between Cowichan Lake and Duncan, this quaint park has two campgrounds—Skutz Falls and Stolz Pool—on the Cowichan River for non-designated camping. No water or wood is provided and there are four pit toilets. The river provides swimming, fishing, and canoeing opportunities.

Dionisio Point

On the northern end of Galiano Island overlooking Porlier Pass is a beautiful quiet campground with 12 walk-in sites a short distance from the shoreline. Pit toilets are provided but there is no water nor wood available. There is, however, an excellent sandy beach. Wildlife viewing opportunities and trails make this one of the more desirable rustic locations. (In 1995 and 1996 a dispute over land development rights closed the access road to the park, so you may want to check the current status of the road).

Loveland Bay

Situated 18 kilometres west of Campbell River this campground is reached via the John Hart Dam gravel road from Highway 28, then by taking the Camp 5 road (gravel). There are 24 fairly undeveloped rustic sites and no fresh water is supplied. Recreational activities include a boat launch, swimming, fishing, and canoeing.

Marble River

This large treed, open campground can be found 30 kilometres from Highway 19 on the paved road to Port Alice. This location has no pit toilets, wood, or fresh water supplied but it does have fishing and hiking opportunities.

Schoen Lake

When I tried to stay here in 1995 the park was closed. BC Parks information states there are ten vehicle/tent sites in addition to tent spots at the five-kilometre Schoen Lake. There is no fresh water nor wood and only two pit toilets. The park is accessed by taking a 12-kilometre gravel road from Highway 19 between Port Hardy and Campbell River. "Schoen" means "beautiful," and the area is noted for excellent scenery and the 1,802-metre summit of Schoen Mountain which is reflected in the lake. Hiking, swimming, fishing, and canoeing can all be enjoyed at this location.

2   VANCOUVER, COAST AND MOUNTAINS

With the highest population density in the province, southwestern BC, Vancouver Coast and Mountains is undoubtedly the most popular region for provincial park camping. Fortunately, 20 provincial parks, all within a four-hour drive from downtown Vancouver, meet the demand for weekend getaways. Even the commute is enjoyable—spectacular scenery can be seen by all those who venture towards their destination. Whether you choose to head north on the meandering Sea to Sky Highway, east on Highway 7 to follow the mighty Fraser River, or via BC Ferries to the Sunshine Coast, your journey will include breathtaking mountain views, clear rivers and streams, forests, fields, and the comforting knowledge that services are never far away.

Sasquatch Provincial Park.

Alice Lake

Location

Alice Lake is situated not far from the community of Brackendale, home to the largest population of bald eagles in North America. Visitors to this campground have a good chance of seeing these splendid birds, but eagles are not the only attraction of this extremely popular park. Alice Lake, easily accessible from Vancouver, is positioned in breathtaking mountain terrain, and has every amenity the camper

Eagle roost. (courtesy Al Nickull)

requires. It is found on Highway 99—the Sea to Sky Highway—13 kilometres north of Squamish, which has all services.

Facilities

Situated in a forest of western hemlock are 88 large, private, shady camping spots suitable for all camping vehicles. The campground is equipped with showers, flush and pit toilets, and a sani-station; it has access for the disabled and accepts reservations.

Recreational activities

There is never a dull moment here as the 397-hectare park has an abundance of activities to keep campers busy. One of the biggest attractions is the series of walking and hiking trails that range in length from half a kilometre to a day's hard walking. One of the most popular is the Four Lakes Trail, which takes hikers around the four warm-water lakes that dominate the area. Swimming, canoeing, and fishing for rainbow trout and Dolly Varden are popular pursuits, and large grassy areas provide venues for ball games. During the summer months interpretive programs are offered.

Additional information

Alice Lake is an excellent base from which to explore Garibaldi Provincial Park, which only offers primitive camping facilities. Garibaldi covers almost 200,000 hectares and during the summer months provides excellent hiking opportunities to alpine meadows, glaciers, mountains, and striking views. Maps of the Garibaldi Provincial Park can be obtained from the Alice Lake campground. Alice Lake is a very popular campground even during the week, and it is frequently full over the peak summer months of July and August, so if you arrive without a reservation during these times make sure you have other options available.

Birkenhead Lake

Location
Six kilometres long, Birkenhead Lake is surrounded by breathtaking snow-capped Coast Moun- tains, blessed with clear beautiful waters, and located only a 3½-hour drive from Vancouver. It is reached by taking Highway 99 to Pemberton, then turning off this road at Mount Currie towards D'Arcy. Just before D'Arcy a 17-kilometre gravel road leads to the park. D'Arcy has a small store while gas and restaurants are found in Mount Currie.

(courtesy BC Parks)

Facilities
Eighty-five camping spaces are available here, and all but a few are located in a beautiful deciduous wooded area with streams running adjacent to them (ideal for keeping your drinks cool on a hot summer day). There is a sani-station but no flush toilets. The park has no wheelchair accessibility. The only other disadvantage is that some spots are near to stagnant water pools, so mosquitoes can be a problem at certain times.

Recreational activities
Birkenhead Lake has a lovely beach and protected swimming area, although the waters themselves, which come directly from the surrounding mountain snow, can be cold. There is a boat launch, and in 1996, canoes could be rented from the BC Parks staff. Fishing for kokanee, whitefish, rainbow trout, and Dolly Varden is reputed to be good as is wildlife watching for moose, black bear, mountain goats, and deer. Ospreys and bald eagles are often seen circling over the waters of the lake. A good trail leads along one side of the lake and is utilized by mountain bikers and walkers.

Additional information
The tranquil location, spectacular scenery, and pleasant drive from the Lower Mainland make this my favourite provincial park for a weekend getaway from Vancouver. When I last visited I canoed around the lake. Be warned that residents of a private development at the opposite end of the lake are not keen on the campers from the provincial park exploring *their* land. Thank goodness we have BC Parks to ensure that access to some of the best scenery in the world is not the privilege of a few.

Brandywine Falls

Location

Stop here and learn from the interpretive signs how this stunning waterfall was formed and how it acquired its unusual name. While the falls themselves are quite spectacular and easily justify an excursion from the highway, this small, functional roadside campground is primarily designed for overnight camping. It is located 47 kilometres north of Squamish (11 kilometres south of Whistler) on the beautiful Sea to Sky Highway. Services can be found in Whistler and Squamish.

Facilities

The 148-hectare park has just 15 camping spots, each quite small and closely packed with low vegetation that offers limited privacy. Only the basic facilities are available here (pit toilets, picnic tables, fire pit, wood, water). The camping spots are quite close to the road, so the noise of passing traffic is easily audible. A railway line also runs close by.

Recreational activities

From this provincial park it is possible to take a short ten-minute hike to a rocky viewpoint to see the impressive 70-metre waterfall and take photographs of Daisy Lake across to the Garibaldi Mountains. Longer trails also exist within the park's boundary. While the recreational pursuits here are somewhat limited, the nearby skiing resort of Whistler offers a host of adventurous pastimes including heliskiing, golfing, hot air ballooning, tennis, horseback riding, and mountain biking.

Additional information

This is very much a roadside campground used out of necessity (but it is quite an enjoyable picnic spot). My advice to anyone travelling north would be to go on to Nairn Falls (40 kilometres north); however, for those travelling south, the popular parks of Alice Lake and Porteau Cove, while preferable, may be full. There are three interesting and distinctive waterfalls on the Sea to Sky Highway. Brandywine is the middle one; to the south is the 335-metre Shannon Falls, the third highest in BC; and to the north is Nairn Falls, where a broad torrent of green water tumbles over 60 metres. Even for those who do not utilize the camping facilities, BC parks provide a host of things to see.

Chilliwack Lake

Location

Today it is rare to find areas of old-growth forest in BC. However, by undertaking a short walk from Chilliwack Lake, visitors can view majestic redcedar trees hundreds of years old. South of Vancouver and situated in the magnificent Coastal Mountains, this popular campground was created in 1973 to protect an area of spectacular beauty in the Lower Mainland mountains. The campground is found 64 kilometres southeast of Chilliwack by taking a turnoff four kilometres south of Highway 1 at Chilliwack and travelling 52 kilometres on a paved and good gravel road. The nearest concentration of services is in Chilliwack; more limited provisions can be found at the Pointa Vista Store, 32 kilometres west of the park.

Facilities

One hundred camping spots are available in the 162-hectare park. Those numbered 1–87 are large, private, and well positioned, with approximately ten being near to the lake. Those numbered 88–100 are close, regimented, and offer little privacy. Only the basic camping facilities are provided here (pit toilets, wood, water, fire pit, picnic tables).

Recreational activities

The park is a delightful place to visit if you enjoy hiking, for a variety of trails lead from the campground. Walkers can choose whether to take an easy six-kilometre return route to the Ecological Reserve with no elevation gain, or the 14 kilometres to Flora Lake with a climb of over 1000 metres. The lake has swimming, boating, and fishing for Dolly Varden, kokanee, rainbow and cutthroat trout and is equipped with a boat launch. The water can, however, be very cold. A playground for children ensures the little ones are well entertained.

Additional information

Almost three kilometres along a logging road that leads from the campground and follows the edge of Chilliwack Lake, is Chilliwack River Ecological Reserve, which was created in 1981 to protect a unique area of old-growth forest featuring large western redcedars. A number of ecological reserves exist in BC, geographically and biologically the most diverse province in the country. They are areas chosen to preserve representative and special natural ecosystems, the fauna and flora. Ecological reserves are used primarily for scientific and educational purposes.

Cultus Lake

Location

In 1995, 28,500 family groups stayed at Cultus Lake, making it the fourth most popular campground in the province. The 656-hectare park

(courtesy BC Parks)

includes both the east and west side of the five-kilometre-long Cultus Lake, from which a spectacular vista of mountains can be seen. "Cultus" means "worthless" in the Chinook language, but the lake's immense popularity suggests that many have found it anything but worthless. Cultus Lake is located 11 kilometres southwest of Chilliwack off Highway 1 on a paved access road. While Chilliwack provides all services, a number of small commercial facilities can be found adjacent to the lake.

Facilities

This campground is the third largest in the province (after Manning and Golden Ears) with 297 spaces in four locations: Maple Bay, Delta Grove, Clear Creek, and Entrance Bay. All spaces are large and well positioned in wooded areas. There are a number of double camping spots, and 18 at Delta Grove are close to the water's edge with their own section of beach. All amenities exist here including flush toilets, sani-station, showers, and access for the disabled. Reservations are accepted.

Recreational activities

Numerous recreational pursuits can be enjoyed. You can catch coho, chinook, chum, pink, and sockeye salmon, rainbow and cutthroat trout, and Dolly Varden if the powerboaters and water skiers do not decide to disturb the tranquillity of the lake. Windsurfing is possible (if the jet skiers are not out in force) as is swimming from lovely sandy beaches. There are a number of hiking trails. The most popular trek is to Teapot Hill, where a good viewpoint rewards your efforts. Some trails permit mountain bikes and horses. For children, a play area has been constructed, and BC Parks offers a number of visitors' programs in the summer months. In the immediate vicinity, commercial outlets have golf, go-carting, canoe rentals, trail rides, and other services.

Additional information

While the setting and facilities here are perfect, the park can become very busy during the summer months, especially on weekends, and somewhat loud if too many powerboats congregate on the lake. Cultus Lake attracts a youthful summer crowd. The best time to stay here is in the spring when the trees are budding, wildflowers are blooming, and the woodlands are alive with bird life attracted to the deciduous forest.

Emory Creek

Location

I love this provincial park for, amongst other things, the unique washroom facilities (see below). This beautiful campground on the banks of the majestic Fraser River is located on the site of Emory City, which in its 1880 heyday boasted 13 streets and a population of over 500 pioneers. Two decades earlier an equal number had worked here after coming in search of gold. If you visit today, all you'll see is a lovely, serene wooded campground. Emory Creek is located beside Highway 1, 18 kilometres north of Hope, six kilometres south of Yale.

Facilities

Nestled in a mixed forest area are 34 large, private camping spots suitable for every type of recreational vehicle. Some spots have views of the water. One of the most distinctive features of this campground is the "flushing thunderboxes"—toilets which from the outside look like pit toilets but which flush. On the two separate occasions that I've stayed in this park these facilities not only flushed but contained small containers of dried flowers and air fresheners. Well done, BC Parks! There is neither sani-station nor showers, nor wheelchair access. The transcontinental railway is adjacent to the park, and the sound of trains, while audible, can be quite soothing to lull you to sleep.

Recreational activities

While there is not a lot to do at Emory Creek, the park seems to attract the retired folks looking for a tranquil spot to spend a few days. There is a small trail, and visitors can fish for salmon in the Fraser, which is easily accessible from a pebbled beach. When I last visited, two grey-haired gentlemen were busy panning for gold, an activity that struck me as an extremely pleasant way to spend an afternoon.

Additional information

This campground has a wonderful feeling about it. Its lack of defined or structured activities makes it particularly appealing to older campers while the well-cared-for and unique washroom facilities are a welcome surprise to seasoned campers who often approach pit toilets (especially in the height of summer) with a deep dread. The area was the site of one of the richest finds during the 1858 gold rush, before prospectors moved farther north. When Simon Fraser first traveled here in 1808, this attractive valley was inhabited by the Coast Salish people, who hunted and fished in the region.

Golden Ears

Location

In 1995, 38,202 camping parties visited Golden Ears, making this well-appointed, large provincial park the most popular campground in BC. Like Cultus Lake and Manning Park, Golden Ears is close to Greater Vancouver. While this proximity may dissuade some from visiting, let me add that whenever I have stayed, even at the height of summer, the park has never felt crowded or busy, and I have thoroughly enjoyed the camping experience. Named either after the twin peaks which shine golden in the sunlight, or, as some locals claim, as a nesting place for eagles—"Golden Eyries"—Golden Ears is located 11 kilometres north of Haney off Highway 7 on a paved access road, an easy 45–60 minute drive from Vancouver. All services are available at Haney, and there are a few additional stores close to the campground itself.

Facilities

Alouette and Gold Creek provide the two well-maintained campgrounds in Golden Ears; the former has 205 spaces, the latter 138. Both have large, private spots within a forested area. All facilities, including showers, flush toilets, a sani-station, and wheelchair access are present. Reservations are accepted.

Recreational activities

The park is blessed with a number of trails suitable for both hikers and horses (horseback riding can be arranged from local facilities). These trails vary from 20-minute interpretive ones to overnight excursions up to the Golden Ears. Fishing for rainbow trout, coastal cutthroat, kokanee, Dolly Varden, and lake trout is popular in Alouette Lake and Alouette River, Pitt Lake, Mike Lake, and Gold Creek. Good swimming beaches are available at Alouette Lake in both the day-use and camping areas. Boating and water-skiing is permitted on the lake away from the swimming area, and canoes can be rented in the park. An adventure playground and the interpretive programs offered throughout the summer keep young ones entertained. BC Parks has a detailed leaflet on all the activities available.

Additional information

The area around Alouette Lake was originally the hunting and fishing ground of the Interior Salish and Coast Salish People. During the early 1900s the area was the primary site for BC's railroad logging operations, and stories are told about the felling of trees up to four metres in diametre in the 1920s. A huge fire that ripped through the area in 1931 stopped the logging operations. Today, Golden Ears is characterized by a second growth of western hemlock, western redcedar, and Douglas-fir, but evidence of the earlier logging is everywhere.

Kilby

Location

If you want a taste of the life experienced by early settlers to the province, visit Kilby Provincial Park and pay a visit to the marvellous nearby museum. One kilometre off Highway 7 at Harrison Falls on the Fraser River is the delectable three-hectare provincial park. Services can be found on the Highway or at Chilliwack, 29 kilometres away.

Facilities

Thirty-eight large camping spots on the river front provide an excellent spot from which to watch the Fraser meander on its course. There are flush and pit toilets but no sani-station, showers, or access for the disabled.

Recreational activities

This campground is ideally located for those who want to explore the surrounding communities of Mission, Agassiz, Chilliwack, and Harrison Hot Springs. It also provides its own attractions in the form of a wide sandy beach and river for boating and swimming. As the campground is positioned near both the Fraser and Harrison Rivers a variety of fishing spots in the immediate vicinity are available where anglers can try their luck for cutthroat and Dolly Varden.

Additional information

One of the biggest attractions of staying here is the Kilby General Store Museum, which is the two-hectare historical site of a general store dating back to the early 1900s. The two-story general store was built in 1904 and operated by the same family up until 1976. This museum contains a small working farm (with pigs, goats, and hens—a delight for children) and orchard in addition to a number of buildings which have been faithfully restored. Guides dressed in period costume provide fascinating details of the development of the area during the turn of the century. Kilby General Store Museum also boasts a gift shop and excellent tea shop serving traditional tea and scones. Both children and adults will find it is easy to pass a number of hours in the museum reading and learning about the Fraser River's colourful past. The photographs of huge sturgeon caught in the Fraser River specifically should not be missed.

The Kilby General Store.

Manning

Location

Manning provides the most campsites (355) of any provincial park and is the second most popular provincial campground (after Golden Ears). In 1995, 35,592 camping groups were recorded. Within three hours of Vancouver (224 kilometres away) and covering over 65,000 hectares of the Cascade Mountains, this is a fantastic area for recreational use. The Highway 3 park entrance is 30 kilometres

(courtesy BC Parks)

east of Hope. Accommodation, gas, food, and other commercial facilities are located in the park.

Facilities

In addition to wilderness camping, there are four campgrounds with, as mentioned above, 355 spots: Hampton (99), Mule Deer (49), Coldspring (64), and Lightning Lake (143). Lightning Lake has showers and flush toilets. All spaces are large and set among trees offering privacy. There is a sani-station near the visitor centre and reservations are accepted.

Recreational activities

Manning Park offers an abundance of things to do and see. Upon arriving, visitors should go to the visitor centre located one kilometre east of the Manning Park Resort to pick up a detailed map of the area. The centre also has human and natural history displays of the park and area. Manning is a hiker's paradise; extensive trail systems meander through the mountains to alpine meadows, waterfalls, and rivers. Some trails are mountain bike accessible, and there are also riding trails and self-guided interpretive trails. Anglers can fish in the Similkameen and Sumallo Rivers for Dolly Varden, rainbow, and cutthroat trout and in Lightning and Strike Lakes. Lightning Lake has a beach, a swimming area, and good canoeing. Powerboats are not permitted anywhere in the park—a rule that ensures a peaceful stay.

Additional information

Manning Park is named after E.C. Manning, Chief Forester of British Columbia from 1935–1940. It is the north end of the Pacific Crest Trail, a six month trek. Almost 4,000 kilometres in length, it runs all the way to Mexico, crossing 24 national forests and seven national parks in the United States. Manning provides a number of delightful hiking alternatives. For an easy 45-minute trail, try the Canyon Trail (two kilometres); for a slightly longer walk, the Lightning Lake Loop (nine kilometres) is appealing. The Lightning Lake Chain Trail is 24 kilometres, but with no elevation gain.

Nairn Falls

Location

One year I stayed here in July, when the temperature was in the high twenties, and I really appreciated the shady canopy this wooded campground offers. Just three kilometres south of Pemberton on Highway 99 and considerably less popular than Alice Lake, its nearest big neighbour to the south, this is an exquisite "laid back" provincial park. Services are conveniently located at Pemberton or at Whistler, 29 kilometres to the south.

Facilities

Eighty-eight spacious forested camping spots are available. Some overlook the canyon; all accommodate the largest recreational vehicle. Facilities include, wood, water, fire pit, picnic tables, pit toilets, and a sani-station.

Recreational activities

Nairn Falls is regularly used by travellers as a picnic spot. An easy 20-minute trail leads to the falls, which tumble 60 metres down into a beautiful canyon of Douglas-fir, cedar, and hemlock. The park contains other trails, but when I visited, the sign-posting left a lot to be desired and some trails were washed out. Fishing is possible in Green River, while a short drive/walk from the park on Highway 99 towards Pemberton there is a lake for swimming, a real luxury on a hot summer's day. The shady, peaceful campground is a perfect location to read and relax, and Nairn Falls gives the impression of offering an almost sophisticated camping experience for those who want to escape from life's pressures.

Additional information

When I stayed here my calm camping environment was infrequently disturbed by the noise of powerboats ascending the rapids to take groups of visitors whitewater rafting. Excursions of this nature can be organized in Pemberton and Whistler. Nairn Falls is an ideal location from which to explore Whistler (and is also considerably cheaper than staying right at the year round resort). It also offers a far more enjoyable environment in which to camp than does its southern neighbour, Brandywine Falls. The lack of recreational pursuits may put some people off (there is little for those with young families to do in the park itself), but for the majority, Nairn Falls is a haven.

Nicolum River

Location

In my opinion, for those who want to camp for more than one night, other provincial park campgrounds in the vicinity (namely Manning and Emory Creek) offer superior camping to Nicolum River. Nonetheless, this is not a bad roadside campground and quite a nice place to stop for a picnic or for one night. On the banks of the river that bears its name, this small campground is often overlooked by those heading to or from its nearest neighbour, Manning. It is located just eight kilometres east of Hope on Highway 3. Services are available at Hope.

Facilities

Claustrophobia will not be a problem here as the campground only has nine spots in a pleasantly wooded area. Only the basic facilities are provided (wood, pit toilets, water, picnic tables, fire pit). The park is quite close to the main road, but the slight noise of traffic is offset to some extent by the rush of the river.

Recreational activities

There is little to do here other than relax and fish for cutthroat, coho, and squawfish on the banks of the river. The town of Hope is less than ten kilometres away and is a pleasant community to wander around. Over the recent past Hope has acquired a number of large carved wooden statues which can be seen in the downtown core. Also a short drive up the Coquihalla Highway and well worth a visit is the Coquihalla Canyon Provincial Recreational Area. It houses a chain of tunnels built for the construction of the Kettle Valley Railway at a cost of $300,000 in 1914. Go, marvel at this engineering feat, walk through the tunnels, and stand in awe as the water crushes down over the rock formations.

Additional information

This is very much a one-night camping spot. Those who seek activity would be better advised to stay at Manning, where there are a multitude of things to do. Be aware that two mountains overshadow Nicoloum River Provincial Park: Tulameen (2,286 metres) and Outram (2,438 metres). These create an early barrier to afternoon sun and promote cold late afternoons and evenings.

Okeover Arm

Location
Over the recent past the waters and islands of this area have become known as a kayaker's dream. Consequently Okeover Arm Provincial Park is a kayaker's campground. At the end of the Sunshine Coast road (Highway 101) overlooking Okeover Arm on the eastern side of the Malaspina Peninsula, this small campground is ideal for campers who plan to kayak in Desolation Sound Marine Park. The park is located 19 kilometres north of Powell River, five kilometres on a paved road from Lund. The small community of Lund has a store and accommodation while Powell River provides all services.

Facilities
Okeover Arm only has five campsites suitable for vehicles and tents and four undeveloped sites on a waterfront setting. Only the basic amenities are available here (wood, pit toilets, water, fire pit, picnic tables).

Recreational activities
The main recreational activities here are canoeing, kayaking, swimming, boating (there is an undeveloped boat launch), and walking in a lightly forested area. As mentioned above, the campground is an ideal base for those who wish to explore Desolation Sound Marine Park, BC's largest marine park, with more than 60 kilometres of shoreline, several islands, and a multitude of bays and coves.

Additional information
There is little to do here if your intention is not to canoe or kayak. Lund seems to be geared to providing a base for this recreational pursuit. When I arrived at Lund I had planned to spend a few hours exploring the community; it could be done in a few minutes. Lund was originally settled in 1895 by two brothers from Sweden and is named after the Swedish city. The renovated hotel which dates back to the turn of the century is the hub of the community.

Porpoise Bay

Location

To reach this campground from the Lower Mainland requires a lovely excursion on BC Ferries to the Sunshine Coast. Take the ferry from Horseshoe Bay to Langdale then Highway 101 to just north of Sechelt where a five-kilometre paved road leads to the campground. Services can be found in Sechelt.

Facilities

Campers here want for nothing. Porpoise Bay has flush and pit toilets, showers, a sani-station, wheelchair access, and accepts reservations. There are 84 large camping spots, including a few double units in second-growth forest of Douglas-fir, western redcedar, western hemlock, and alder.

Recreational activities

This popular park and campground offers a wide sandy beach and a protected swimming area ideal for family camping. A large number of grassy areas great for ball games are a feature here, and there are small trails, one of which leads to Angus Creek, a salmon spawning waterway for chum and coho. One of the park's main draws is as a base for kayakers who use it to explore the many coves and inlets of the surrounding area. Interpretive programs are offered in the summer.

Additional information

Porpoise Bay is near to the Sechelt Inlet's Provincial Marine Recreational Area, which includes eight wilderness campsites located in the sheltered waters of the Sechelt Inlet—a paddler's delight. The area is also rich in marine life. Therefore, although Porpoise Bay is popular, especially for families, those who choose to paddle away can easily find a rich tranquillity amongst beautiful west coast scenery.

Thrill of a lifetime– kayaking with a whale.
(courtesy Sea Dog Sailing & Kayaking)

Porteau Cove

Location

The views from this campground on the fantastic Sea to Sky Highway (Route 99) are stunning if the weather is good, and for this reason alone every attempt should be made to stop here. Although almost impossible to see from the road, Porteau Cove is an enchanting roadside campground with an astounding vista of Howe Sound, the most southerly fjord in North America. Thirty-eight kilometres north of Vancouver, just over eight kilometres south of Britannia Beach, Porteau Cove provides a haven for campers and day trippers. Britannia Beach has food; gas and other provisions are available in Squamish.

Facilities

The campground brags 59 vehicle camping spots in addition to 15 walk-in sites and all amenities (showers, flush toilets, sani-station, wheelchair access, and reservations). Some spots look directly onto the water's edge over to the mountains on Vancouver Island, and while not as large as those in other provincial parks, have privacy awarded by the surrounding Sitka spruce trees. The campground is set away from the road so traffic noise is not a problem, but the railway does run close by, and a number of trains pass by during the day.

Recreational activities

One of the biggest attractions at this location is scuba diving. Three ships have been sunk in the nearby waters to attract marine life and create a destination for diving enthusiasts as well as to provide entertainment for the rest of us who just want to watch funny rubber-clad individuals plunge into the cool waters. Away from the diving area it is possible to swim in the waters of Howe Sound and to fish. The public boat launch at Porteau Cove is the only one between Squamish and Horseshoe Bay. The park is an extremely popular camping and picnic spot for people travelling along the Highway. Interpretive programs are offered during the summer.

Additional information

This park can be easily accessed by train from Vancouver, so those living within Vancouver who do not possess a vehicle can still appreciate its splendor. The Mining Museum at Britannia Beach is well worth a visit if you have time. Visitors are given hard hats and taken on a tour which includes a rail trip underground and a demonstration of past mining machinery. Britannia Beach also has a large number of arts and craft shops and cafes to visit. Porteau Cove is a *very* popular location, so expect to be disappointed if planning to camp there without a reservation during the peak months of July and August.

Roberts Creek

Location

If you want to spend your time relaxing, beachcombing, and staring out to sea to look for whales, then stop at Roberts Creek. With fantastic views of the Georgia Strait and beyond to the mountains of Vancouver Island, this campground is found 12 kilometres north of Gibsons on Highway 101. From the Lower Mainland, visitors must take a beautiful ferry ride from Horseshoe Bay to Langdale. Services are available at Gibsons or Sechelt, 15 kilometres to the north.

Facilities

Camping facilities are situated in a lightly forested area of second growth Douglas-fir and western redcedar. There are 25 spaces, a sani-station but no flush toilets or showers. The park is wheelchair accessible. It is quite near the main road and noise from traffic may be a problem for some.

Recreational activities

Beachcombing is a favourite distraction here. At low tide a cobblestone beach reveals sea stars, mussels, oysters and an array of marine life. From the beach it is also possible to see whales, seals, and sea lions, but don't count on it—they were somewhat elusive when I visited. Although the waters tend to be cold, swimming and fishing are also enjoyed by some.

Additional information

The area of coastline from Langdale to Lund is called the Sunshine Coast because of its warm summers and mild winters. Precipitation here is almost 170 mm less than in Vancouver, making the Sunshine Coast a desirable place to live. Roberts Creek campground is located on one of the busiest sections of the area. Those who prefer more tranquil surroundings are advised to travel on and take the second ferry from Earls Cove to Saltery Bay; the northern section of the Sunshine Coast is considerably quieter than the southern section.

All government parks boast excellent signage and direction.

Rolley Lake

Location

Some parks are criticized for being too big, some for being too small. In my opinion, Rolley Lake is not only a perfect size, but is easily accessible from Vancouver, has a delightful setting, boasts a number of recreational activities, and is well equipped. It is located 23 kilometres northwest of Mission (70 kilometres east of Vancouver). Although well sign-posted from Highway 7, the location is a little confusing. In Maple Ridge turn off Highway 7 north at 287th on to the Dewdney Trunk Road, turn right on to Bell Road where you then make a left turn towards the park. The road is paved all the way to the park. Maple Ridge and Mission both have comprehensive services.

Facilities

This popular campground has 64 spacious units set in a woodland area of western hemlock and mature vine maple awarding privacy and shade. The facilities are among the best provided by BC Parks and include showers, sani-station, flush and pit toilets, and wheelchair access. Reservations are accepted.

Recreational activities

The 115 hectares of Rolley Lake Provincial Park provide a relaxing environment for campers. The lake is surrounded by forest, and because powerboats are prohibited, it is a peaceful place to relax, canoe, swim, and fish (primarily for rainbow trout). There are a number of short walks: one leads to a waterfall; another leads around the lake, includes a section of boardwalk, and takes about 90 minutes. Children can have fun in the play area, and interpretive programs are offered in the summer months. Rolley Lake is also a good place for observing bird life.

Additional information

Rolley Lake, which takes its name from Fanny and James Rolley, who settled here in 1888, has played an active part in the logging industry of BC. In the early part of the century the lake stored shingle bolts destined for a mill located at Ruskin, five kilometres away. In the 1930s when all the old-growth forest had gone, it became home to a small Japanese-Canadian logging operation harvesting Douglas-fir. BC Parks acquired it in 1961, and today it provides a tranquil environment for those who wish to escape the main centres of population. The park has the advantage of being relatively small and yet supplying all facilities. These characteristics, together with its tranquil location and proximity to the Lower Mainland, ensure a pleasant camping experience.

Saltery Bay

Location

Come and see Canada's first underwater statue at Saltery Bay, but remember to bring all the correct diving equipment! Saltery Bay Provincial Park is located about 27 kilometres south of Powell River on the north shore of Jervis Inlet. Visitors must take two delightful short ferry rides, one from Horseshoe Bay to Langdale, then drive on Highway 101 to Earls Cove and catch the second ferry to Saltery Bay. The land and sea route from the Lower Mainland and the ocean-view scenery at Saltery Bay make this camping excursion a real delight. Thirty kilometres north, Powell River has all services.

Facilities

In an evergreen forest are 42 large, private camping units. The campground has a sani-station but only pit toilets and no showers. It is wheelchair accessible and accepts reservations.

Recreational activities

In addition to the superb ocean-view scenery, the shallow offshore waters of the park are the biggest attraction here. Scuba divers are enticed to the area by the variety of marine life, underwater cover, and shipwrecks (there is also disabled diver access). To the delight of many divers, a three-metre bronze mermaid has been sunk under the water at Mermaid Cove. This art form has the honour of being Canada's first underwater statue. For those who do not dive, the park offers a number of alternatives, including beaches for swimming and sunbathing, a two-kilometre hiking trail to Little Saltery Falls, the chance to see killer whales, seals, and sea lions who occasionally bask in the area, and salmon fishing from April to October. What more could you ask?

Additional information

Saltery Bay is named after the fish saltery located here at the turn of the century; prior to that time, native people inhabited the area. Today, the mounds of seashells on the beach are evidence of their existence. This popular diving area has been featured by *National Geographic* and is an excellent spot from which to explore the Sunshine Coast.

(courtesy BC Parks)

Sasquatch

Location

In commenting on the popularity of Sasquatch, one traveller suggests using contrary thinking: Head there on a Monday of a holiday weekend when the crowds are on their way home. With four pristine lakes, including the freshwater fjord of massive Harrison Lake, and over 1,220 hectares of land, it is easy to see why this park is popular. The park provides a vast expanse to explore amongst beautiful mountain scenery. Sasquatch is located six kilometres north of Harrison Hot Springs off Highway 7. All services are found at Harrison.

Facilities

The 177 camping units are set in an area of second-growth deciduous forest and are divided into two areas. Hicks Lake campground has 68 spots, some close to the lake, while the Lakeside and Bench campgrounds are nearer to Deer Lake. There are flush and pit toilets and a sani-station but no showers. The park accepts reservations but is not wheelchair accessible.

Recreational activities

The four lakes at this location (Harrison, Hicks, Deer, and Trout) vary in size and in the recreational pursuits they offer. Harrison and Hicks Lakes permit powerboats, while at Deer Lake only electric motors are allowed. Trout Lake prohibits powerboats and consequently is ideal for canoeing and kayaking. Trout fishing here is reputed to be excellent. A number of trails lead around the park, and some of these are suitable for mountain bikes. Two beach locations ensure sun-worshipping opportunities—one is at the southern end of Hicks Lake and one by the group camping area. From this second location it is possible to swim to two small forested islands ideal for exploring. A play area for children is located at the Lakeside campground, and interpretive programs are offered during the summer. The nearby town of Harrison Hot Springs, famous for its mineral pools, holds a sandcastle-building contest in August.

Additional information

The name "Sasquatch" is an English interpretation of the Coast Salish word "Sasqac." The Sasqac is a mythical creature believed to possess a certain type of spirit which should be avoided—a sort of Bigfoot. Local native bands still report sightings of the Sasquatch around Harrison River, so be warned! This area is spectacular in the fall when the colours are at their height; fall is also a good time to visit Harrison Hot Springs, which can become very busy during the peak summer months.

Skagit Valley

Location

For me the words "Skagit Valley" and "mosquitoes" are synonymous. Had I visited when these insects were not biting, Skagit Valley would probably rank as one of my top ten campgrounds. Encompassing over 32,500 hectares this park is in the Northern Cascades. West of Hope, a gravel road leads 32 kilometres to Skagit Valley but the main camping area is an additional 26 kilometres on bumpy gravel. Once at Ross Lake (the main campground), the scenery is awesome. The nearest services are back at Hope, so stock up before making the journey.

Facilities

Two campgrounds offer 132 sites; 44 are at Silvertip, adjacent to the Skagit River near the park's entrance, and the rest are at Ross Lake. Silvertip is set among trees; Ross Lake tends to be more open, some near the water's edge. There is no sani-station nor wheelchair access, and facilities are basic ones found in BC parks (water, wood, fire pit, picnic tables, pit toilets).

Recreational activities

At Silvertip trails lead along the Skagit River. Ross Lake has hiking trails, a boat launch, an adventure playground for children. The lake is surrounded by fantastic snow-covered mountains. The Skagit River is one of the best fly-fishing streams in North America and the most productive stream in the Lower Mainland. Fishing for Dolly Varden, char, eastern brook trout, and cutthroat trout is good. Wildlife here includes deer, black bear, cougar, coyote, mink, and raccoons. There is also a wide array of birds.

Additional information

Over 20 years ago a public protest saved the valley from being flooded by a Seattle hydro company. Today, the water level at Ross Lake is controlled by a hydro dam in Washington State and is subject to fluctuations. As I bounced along the 58 kilometres of gravel road I cursed the fact that the park entrance was so far from the campground and this information is not conveyed to the uninitiated. Then I beheld the mountain scenery that surrounds the lake and suddenly the journey was worth it. I did not stay the night due to the mosquitoes out in force on that July day.

Additional Campgrounds

Silver Lake

Found on the approach road to Skagit Valley, this campground on the edge of a small lake has 30 spots, some of which are located in pull-ins at the side of the gravel road. Although the site is blessed with some beautiful scenery, there is neither water nor firewood and there are only two pit toilets. Recreational activities are confined to swimming and fishing in the lake. When I visited Silver Lake groups of teenagers seemed to be very well established. My advice would be to travel on to Skagit Valley rather than camp here. If you do not like gravel roads, try nearby Emory Creek.

3 Okanagan Similkameen

Make sure you pack the sun screen if your vacation plans include a trip to the Okanagan. The fruit (and wine) basket of the country enjoys over 2,000 hours of sunshine a year, making it a rich producer of crops and the envy of many other areas of the country. This region of the province features miles upon miles of orchards and vineyards, crystal-clear lakes, warm-hearted communities, and undulating countryside. The Okanagan-Similkameen area incorporates Highway 3 from Kettle Valley to Princeton, Highway 33, Highway 97, Highway 5A south of Aspen Grove to Princeton, and Highway 6. So remember to wear your sunglasses, and have fun exploring the eighteen provincial parks that offer camping in the Okanagan.

Bear Creek Provincial Park.

Allison Lake

Location
On the relatively quiet Highway 5A at the southern end of Allison Lake is an enchanting little 23-hectare campground, perfect for those with time on their hands. Services can be found at Princeton, 28 kilometres south.

Facilities
Twenty-four large, well-positioned camping spaces exist in a lovely forested area. The sites are suitable for every type of vehicle, and although some are quite close to the road, there is not a lot of traffic. All the basic amenities exist (fire pit, wood, water, picnic tables, pit toilets).

Recreational activities
The primary recreational activities here centre around beautiful Allison Lake and include swimming, fishing, canoeing, and kayaking. The lake is bordered by aspen trees, and the area is particularly attractive during the fall when the trees turn golden and red and present fantastic photographic opportunities.

Additional information
This is one of the better roadside campgrounds primarily used for overnight camping. Highway 5A between Kamloops and Princeton is a lovely quiet route on which to appreciate the scenery of the Okanagan. And for those who have the time, it is far more pleasant to travel than the busy Coquihalla Highway. The route is 118 kilometres longer than the main highway but avoids the long, steep hills of the Coquihalla as well as the ten-dollar toll fee. Be prepared for little development and a scenic drive if heading south from the campground as the road follows Allison Creek to Princeton.

On the water, children should always wear lifejackets.
(courtesy Dennis Hurd)

Bear Creek

Location
Go to sleep to the sound of a tree frog at this popular 167-hectare campground. Bear Creek exhibits a variety of geological features, including sandy beaches and spectacular canyons and waterfalls. These features are supplemented with a diversity of vegetation, which encourages wildlife populations. Bear Creek is situated to the north of the Okanagan, nine kilometres west of Kelowna (where services are found) on the western side of Okanagan Lake off Highway 97 on a paved access road.

Facilities
Bear Creek provides 80 camping spots and every type of camping service including flush and pit toilets, a sani-station, showers, and access for the disabled. Sites accommodate all recreational vehicles and there are a number of double spots. Some of the more desirable spots overlook Lambley (Bear) Creek where campers can be lulled to sleep by the sound of the trickling waters (not recommended for those with weak bladders). Reservations are accepted.

Recreational activities
This stunning location facilitates a variety of recreational pursuits. The beach is over 400 metres in length, ideal for swimming and sunbathing. The lake has rainbow trout, whitefish, and kokanee and boating potential. In addition to a number of smaller interpretive trails, over 15 kilometres of well-maintained hiking trails exist; some of which lead to views of the lake and canyon. Remember to pack the camera as there are excellent photographic opportunities. Children can enjoy an adventure playground; there is a horseshoe pit, and BC Parks staff offer interpretive programs in the summer. Bear Creek is home to a vast array of wildlife, including swallows, hawks, and owls. Tree frogs can be heard in the spring, and rattlesnakes live in the vicinity but are rarely seen.

Additional information
In the early fall, kokanee can be observed spawning in the lower reaches of the creek. The quality of the creek's water was recognized by the Kelowna Brewing Company, who many years ago established a brewery nearby. This park is extremely popular in the summer months, but if the location is full when you visit, the BC Parks gatehouse staff can advise you where to go.

Bromley Rock

Location

Set aside a striding rock bluff on the Similkameen River, 21 kilometres east of Princeton on Highway 3, is the riverside campground of Bromley Rock Provincial Park. In staying here, campers trace the footsteps of the early pioneers who came in search of gold and other minerals. Services are located at Princeton.

Facilities

The campground has 17 spots set in a forested area near the Similkameen River. All the basic facilities exist here (fire pit, water, wood, picnic tables, pit toilets) and the park is wheelchair accessible.

Recreational activities

The river supplies a pleasant place for swimming in delightful cool swimming holes, and there is fishing potential. When I visited, local young male adventurers could be observed "tubing" downstream to Stemwinder Provincial Park, an activity not recommended for the uninitiated. Just outside the park, hiking trails lead to fantastic views of the Similkameen Valley. The nearby town of Princeton was named in 1860 to commemorate the visit of the Prince of Wales that year. Princeton has a pioneer museum with displays of clothing, mining exhibits, and furnishings. Artifacts from the native Salish people and Chinese immigrants who played a major role in the early development of mining and the railway are also on show.

Additional information

This campground is only 14 kilometres from Stemwinder Provincial Park, which is slightly larger in capacity and may provide an alternative should Bromley Rock be full. The area was originally inhabited by the Salish and Shuswap people who have left traces of their existence in the locality. More recently the area was explored by miners and trappers.

Bear Creek Provincial Park.

Conkle Lake

Location
If you are looking for a back-country retreat to get away from the crowds and you can endure a bumpy road, this is the place for you. The campground is in a beautiful location amidst the Okanagan Highlands, but BC Parks warns that the access route along gravel twisting roads is not suitable for large motor homes or towed trailers. Consequently, those travelling in these types of vehicles may wish to choose another spot. The park is reached by three gravel access road points: from Highway 33 at Westbridge it is found after driving for 16 kilometres on a gravel road; from Highway 3, six kilometres east of Bridesville a 26-kilometre gravel road leads to the site; and from Highway 97 at Okanagan Falls a 35-kilometre gravel road can be taken. Services are available at Westbridge and at the junction of Highway 3 and Highway 33.

Facilities
There are 34 private camping spots located in a forest of western larch, lodgepole pine, alder, and willow on the northwest corner of the lake. Only the basic facilities provided by BC Parks exist (pit toilets, picnic tables, wood, water, cooking pit). There is no sani-station.

Recreational activities
Conkle Lake has a beautiful beach from which it is possible to sunbathe, swim, or fish for rainbow trout. A steep dropoff, however, means non-swimmers and children should be cautious. There is a boat launch and a number of hiking trails that lead from the campground. One of these includes a beautiful multi-tiered waterfall.

Additional information
The park is named after an early settler to the Kettle Valley, W.H. Conkle. The fact this park is relatively difficult to access by the RV population may suggest it is a campground only for four-wheel-drivers and their passengers to enjoy. When I visited, there were quite a few large recreational vehicles that had obviously successfully managed the route and whose owners were enjoying the beautiful Okanagan scenery.

(courtesy BC Parks)

Ellison

Location

If diving is your game then Ellison Park should be your aim. In addition to the diving opportunities it provides, Ellison is an excellent spot for a family vacation. Set on the northeastern shore of Okanagan Lake and encompassing 200 hectares between the Thompson Plateau and the Monashee Mountains, the park is reached by travelling 16 kilometres southwest of Vernon on Highway 97. All services are available in Vernon.

Facilities

The park has 54 spacious, well-appointed sites set in a natural forest of Douglas-fir and ponderosa pine and suitable for every size of recreational vehicle. There are flush and pit toilets but no sani-station or showers. The park is wheelchair accessible and reservations are accepted.

Recreational activities

Ellison Provincial Park is home to Canada's only freshwater dive park. A number of objects and artifacts have been sunk here to attract fish and create a diving haven for the rubber-clad enthusiasts of dark, cold waters. If diving is not your passion there are a wide array of other activities to enjoy, including six kilometres of hiking trails which take visitors to many of the park's natural features and viewpoints. (Watch out for porcupines often seen on the popular Ellison Trail.) Two protected beach areas ideal for swimming and sunbathing are equipped with changing facilities and an outdoor shower. Fishermen can try their luck for large carp, burbot, kokanee, and trout, and while there is no boat launch in the park, one is located six kilometres to the north. BC Parks offers interpretive programs throughout the summer months, one of the most popular being an evening of star-gazing as the clear Okanagan skies offer excellent opportunities for astronomy.

Additional information

Ellison is in the heart of the fruit growing region of the province, and as they have done since the 1800s, orchards, ranches, and farms dominate the area. This park provides an excellent base from which to explore the North Okanagan and to savour the produce of the region.

(courtesy BC Parks)

Fintry

Location

This is the baby of BC Parks and therefore has yet to be appreciated by many (including myself). Ideally situated for exploring the Okanagan and found in one of the region's few remaining natural areas, Fintry started to register campers in 1996. The park is adjacent to Okanagan Lake, 32 kilometres north of Kelowna and 24 kilometres south of Vernon. It is clearly sign-posted from Highway 97 on eight kilometres of paved access road. Services are available at Kelowna and Vernon.

Facilities

Camping facilities in this new addition include flush toilets and showers, but there is no access for the disabled. Fifty camping spots are available and reservations are accepted.

Recreational activities

Within close proximity to the campground is a beautiful two-kilometre sandy beach, ideal for swimming, sunbathing, and family activities. Although no boat launch is provided in the park itself, the regional district public boat launch is found one kilometre from the park's boundary. Fishing in the warm waters of Okanagan Lake can be rewarding, while the Shorts Creek Canyon Trail provides hikes that offer the opportunity to view white-tailed deer and bighorn sheep as well as a variety of birds. BC Parks warns that caution should be exercised on sections of the trails, which are quite narrow in places and near to steep cliffs.

Additional information

The park is a heritage site occupying the former Fintry Estate. Its history dates back to the last century when fur dealers traded with the native inhabitants of the area. In 1909 James Cameron, originally from Scotland, purchased the land and called it Fintry. He built many of the buildings that exist today, including the manor house and farm buildings. Fintry has the advantage of being located in a popular area, but because of its youth as a camping haven it is yet to be fully exploited by the camping public. It will not be long before this situation changes.

Haynes Point

Location

It is a great shame that this popular campground is not larger. Whenever I have attempted to stay in its idyllic setting it has always been full. Haynes Point is located at the southern end of the Okanagan River Valley, in the rainshadow of the Cascade Mountains on Osoyoos Lake, just two kilometres from Osoyoos on Highway 97.

Facilities

It is of little wonder Haynes Point is a popular retreat as all of the 41 camping spots are located on a narrow sandspit with over half having direct access onto the beach. There are both flush and pit toilets but no sani-station or showers. The park is accessible by wheelchair. Reservations are accepted.

Recreational activities

The deep Okanagan River Valley formed by glacier erosion receives less than 35 centimetres of rain per annum and is Canada's only true desert. The lake is reputed to be the warmest in the country, making it a magnet for swimming, boating (there is a boat launch), and for rainbow trout and bass fishing. The warm climate and lack of precipitation promotes desert-loving plants such as ponderosa pine, bear cacti, sage grass, and greasewood, which in turn provides a habitat for a wide array of bird, animal, and reptile life, including species such as the spadefoot toad, burrowing owl, and desert night snake that are unique to the area. Visitor's programs held in the summer give details of these animals and more.

Additional information

The park is named after Judge John Carmichael Haynes who came to Osoyoos in 1866 and became a renowned legal authority and land owner. According to legend, he brought law and order to the goldfields of Whitehorse Creek, near Cranbrook. Native people lived, hunted, and fished in the area; two archeological sites in the park provide proof of this long history. Haynes Point is an extremely popular location during the peak summer months with the climate also ensuring a pleasant stay for those who choose to visit in the spring and fall. Some of the Okanagan's finest vineyards and fruit farms are found in this region. From May to November fresh fruit and vegetable stands at the side of the highway ensure produce is readily available for campers to enjoy around an open fire.

Inkaneep

Location

Inkaneep is an ideal spot from which to experience the excellent local fruit and wine. On the shores of the Okanagan River, this 21-hectare campground is found six kilometres north of Oliver on Highway 97. Services are found in Oliver.

Facilities

Inkaneep offers seven camping spots more suitable for tents than RVs, set in a shady oasis of cottonwood trees on the edge of the Okanagan River. Only the basic facilities are available here (pit toilets, picnic tables, water, wood, and cooking pit).

Recreational activities

From this campground it is possible to fish in the Okanagan River and to canoe (although it is quite a trek from the campground to the water). The arid desert habitat around the park is home to many species of wildlife, consequently one of the main activities here is bird-watching as the area is home to blackheaded grosbeak, American redstart, northern oriole, yellow warbler, Lewis's woodpecker, and warbling vireo. An ecological reserve is located near by.

Additional information

Just south of Oliver is a "pocket desert." When I visited, it was somewhat difficult to find as there are no signposts. However, once discovered, the area is interesting as it supports subtropical flora and fauna such as cactus, horned lizards, rattlesnakes, and burrowing owls. The town of Oliver was established in 1921 under a land grant by the BC Premier John Oliver in a settlement for veterans from the First World War. Now it is known for housing some of the best wineries in the country, tours of which are available to visitors. Be sure you make time to explore the local caves and perhaps purchase a bottle of wine for savouring around the campfire.

Kettle River

Location

Between 1860 and 1864 this region was worked by over 500 miners who scoured the gravels for gold. Today it provides a more tranquil setting for camping enthusiasts. Named after the river that runs through it, Kettle River Provincial Park is located five kilometres north of Rock Creek on Highway 33. Some services (pub, gas, store, accommodation) are located at Rock Creek.

Facilities

At a bend on the west bank of the river are 53 well-spaced camping spots nestled in an area of ponderosa pine and birchgrass, and suitable for every size of recreational vehicle. In addition to the basic facilities offered, there is a sani-station. There are no flush toilets or access for the disabled.

Recreational activities

The Kettle Valley Railway discontinued its service in the early 1970s, and in 1979-80 the track was removed between Midway and Penticton. The abandoned route runs through the park and has created an excellent hiking and biking trail. From the park it is possible to fish, swim, and canoe. On the eastern banks of the river remains of gold and silver mines can be seen— evidence of the pioneers who travelled and worked in the area at the turn of the century. Excellent opportunities exist for the photographer and artist in this locale, while many resurrect the past by panning for gold.

Additional information

For those who decide not to cook over an open fire there is an interesting although limited collection of eateries at Rock Creek including a pub and good breakfast cafes. Rock Creek dates back to 1857 when a prospector called CharleS Dietz started a gold rush here. Large quantities of gold were never found but copper was. During the winter the area is very popular with cross-country skiers and snowshoers.

Mabel Lake

Location

Mabel Lake is perfect for those who want to appreciate the Okanagan from a "cooler" vantage point. Somewhat off the beaten track, it is a lovely 182-hectare provincial park between the Thompson Plateau to the west and the Monashee Mountains to the east. Temperatures here tend to be cooler than in many other areas of the Okanagan and provide a pleasant respite from the summer heat. The campground is found 76 kilometres northeast of Vernon. Travel on Highway 6 to Lumby, then take a mostly paved road for 35 kilometres. Services are available at Lumby and there is also a small marine store by the campground.

Facilities

Camping here is divided into two campgrounds, the Monashee ground and the Trinity campground, which provide a total of 81 well-situated spaces in a wooded setting. There is a sani-station but no flush toilets or showers. The park is wheelchair accessible.

Recreational activities

A 2100-metre shoreline that includes a lovely beach with a safe swimming area provides access to the waters of 35-kilometre-long Mabel Lake. Fishing is good both from the shore and in the deeper waters where anglers can hope to catch rainbow trout, Dolly Varden, lake trout, kokanee, and Chinook salmon. Water-skiing and boating is popular, and the nearby marina offers boat rentals. The area is attractive to canoeists who paddle down the Shuswap River just south of the park. BC Parks staff at Mabel Lake offer interpretive programs during the summer months, and for those who like to see more unusual wildlife, painted turtles can be observed in Taylor Creek. The park also has a one-hour interpretive trail.

Additional information

The adjacent area offers interesting alternatives to the recreational activities found in the park. The road between Lumby and Mabel Lake takes travellers through the distinctive landscape of ranches and farmland. Wilsey Dam has a picnic spot with trails leading to the awe-inspiring Shuswap Falls.

(courtesy Dennis Hurd)

Okanagan Falls

Location

Native legend recalls how the waters here once fell with "a voice like thunder" and a spray as white as cherry blossom. Today, development has ensured that visitors cannot experience the original natural beauty of the falls, but instead there exists a lovely provincial park. Okanagan Falls, known as "OK Falls" to the locals, is found at the community which bears its name on Highway 97 south of Skaha Lake. All basic services can be found here.

Facilities

The picturesque campground with 25 camping spots is set amongst a forest of deciduous trees just above the Okanagan River. It is wheelchair accessible and provides flush and pit toilets but no sani-station or showers.

Recreational activities

Like the two other provincial parks in the immediate vicinity (Vaseux Lake and Inkaneep) the area is rich in bird and animal life and therefore a favourite location for nature study and photography. A species of small sonar-equipped bats are found here in addition to a wealth of other birds and animals. Fishing is possible in the Okanagan River and the park has horseshoe pits. For those looking for a beach and swimming, Christie Memorial Provincial Park, which has 200 metres of beach and good swimming, is located just north of Okanagan Falls. As the area is rich in grapevines, tours of the local wineries provide an interesting distraction.

Additional information

Anyone looking for spectacular waterfalls will be disappointed as Okanagan Falls have been reduced to rapids because of rock blasting for water control in the area. The museum at Okanagan Falls is housed in a 1909 restored prefabricated building which was ordered from a catalogue, shipped in pieces, and assembled here. It contains artifacts and memorabilia of the pioneer Bassett family.

Okanagan Lake

Location

In 1995 over 21,000 camping parties regis-tered at Okanagan Lake, making it the most popular camping location in the Okanagan. Like other provincial parks such as Haynes Point and Bear Creek, Okanagan Lake is very popular in the peak summer months of July and

(courtesy The BC Adventure Network)

August. Located 24 kilometres north of Penticton between Peachland and Summerland, where services can be found, this park has fantastic panoramic views of the Okanagan Mountains and lake.

Facilities

The park has 168 vehicle/tent campsites, 80 in the north campground and 88 in the south, some with views of the lake. I prefer the camping spots in the north campground, which are better spaced and less regimented than those in the south. Both are set in an unusual forest area (see below). Each campground has showers and flush and pit toilets. The south campground has a sani-station and boat launch. The park is wheelchair accessible and reservations are accepted.

Recreational activities

With over one kilometre of beach, Okanagan Lake is a paradise for swimmers, sunbathers, anglers, and water sports enthusiasts. The lake is popular for windsurfing and sailing, and for those who prefer other activities a number of small hiking trails exist in the 98-hectare park. BC Parks runs visitor program activities throughout the summer months from late June to Labour Day. One of the unique features of the park is an arboretum of over 10,000 exotic trees, including Russian olive, Chinese elm, Norway, Manitoba and Silver maples, and Red, Blue and Mountain ash. This woodland enhances the birdlife so keep your eyes pealed for hummingbirds, larks, and woodpeckers, which can be easily seen. Fantastic photographic opportunities.

Additional information

Across the lake is Okanagan Mountain Provincial Park, a 10,000-hectare undeveloped Okanagan Basin wilderness stretching from the lakeshore to the top of the mountains. As mentioned above, Okanagan Lake is a very popular camping location, and you may well be disappointed if you arrive without a reservation in the peak summer months. If you do find a spot, you are guaranteed to have a good time.

Otter Lake

Location

Literature from BC Parks states that Otter Lake is ideal for "old fashioned camping," whatever that may be. This provincial park is found 47 kilometres northwest of Princeton off Highway 5A on 32 kilometres of paved road near the small towns of Tulameen and Coalmont, which have services.

Facilities

Otter Lake boasts 45 beautifully spaced, large camping spots on the northwest shore of the lake, some with views of the water. There are flush and pit toilets but no sani-station or showers. The park is wheelchair accessible and accepts reservations.

Recreational activities

The five-kilometre Otter Lake provides the main recreational activity in the form of fishing for lake trout, swimming from a warm beach, and boating (a boat launch is provided). There is also a horseshoe pit. The surrounding area is home to a variety of animal life including otter, beaver, red squirrel, mountain goat, cougar, and grizzly bear, but do not expect to see them all on your first visit!

Additional information

Otter lake is an ideal base from which to explore the mining history of the Tulameen region. The town of Tulameen, which is a native name meaning "red earth," is located five kilometres south of the campground. Tulameen was first used by Indians for hunting and fishing and then explored by gold miners in the last century. The Hudson's Bay Company used a road that passed through Tulameen and called the settlement "encampment des femmes" as it was populated primarily by women waiting for their men to return from trapping and hunting. The town of Coalmont just south of the park is another goldrush town; in 1925 it produced 100,000 tons of coal, making it the region's largest producer. By 1940 the mine was exhausted and most residents moved away. Today Coalmont contains a cafe, a general store, and a hotel dating back to 1912.

Stemwinder

Location

Between 1904 and 1955, 47 million dollars in gold was taken from the mountains adjacent to Stemwinder Provincial Park, and rumour has it that there is still some left . . . so what are you waiting for? "There's gold in them there hills!" This small (four-hectare) roadside campground is very much geared towards overnight stops. It is found 35 kilometres east of Princeton on Highway 3 next to Hedley. Services are available in Hedley.

Facilities

The campground provides 27 spots on the banks of the Similkameen River. Only the basic amenities found in BC Parks are available (water, pit toilets, picnic tables, fire pit and wood), and the camping spots are quite close to the road, so expect the noise of traffic. The park does have access for the disabled.

Recreational activities

Because this campground is geared towards overnight camping as opposed to long-term recreational camping, it provides limited recreational activities. The waters of the Similkameen River can be fished but are fast-flowing. Caution must be taken by those who wish to swim but are not strong swimmers. Alternatively you could try your luck at panning for gold, an activity which started here at the turn of the century. Be careful to avoid the poison ivy found along the river bank.

Additional information

When visiting this area it is worth turning off Highway 3 to explore the back roads and some of the older architecture in the quaint Okanagan community of Hedley. Hedley dates back to the beginning of this century when the Nickel Plate Mine, one of BC's first hardrock mining operations, was established 1,200 metres above the town. The mine operated from 1904–1956, producing gold, silver, and copper.

Visit the old Grist Mill at Keremeos, east of Hedley. (courtesy The BC Adventure Network)

Vaseux Lake

Location

"Vaseux" is French for "muddy." This shallow, four-kilometre-long, one-kilometre-wide, weedy lake is one of Canada's foremost birding areas and a real magnet for ornithologists. Between the highway and the lake sits Vaseux Lake Provincial Park, a 12-hectare roadside campground. It is located four kilometres south of Okanagan Falls, 25 kilometres south of Penticton.

Facilities

This 12-spot campground surrounded by cliffs contains all the basic amenities found in BC Parks (pit toilets, picnic tables, wood, water, fire pit) together with wheelchair accessibility. There is no sani-station. As the highway is close to the campground, noise from traffic is audible.

Recreational activities

This area attracts ornithologists and wildlife enthusiasts. A variety of grasses, weeds, and willow vegetation provide a home for birds and animals. Waterfowl and birds of the area include trumpeter swans, widgeons, Canada geese, wood ducks, blue winged teal, chuckar partridge, wrens, swifts, woodpeckers, and dippers. Californian bighorn sheep inhabit the cliffs near the park, while smaller mammals in the area include beavers, muskrats, deer, mice, rattlesnakes, and turtles. The lake is excellent for fishing in both winter and summer and yields largemouth bass, rainbow trout, and carp. The park is equipped with a beach for sunbathing and swimming. There is no boat launch and powerboats are prohibited, but canoeing and kayaking are permitted on the lake.

Additional information

Near the park is the Canadian Wildlife Service wildlife sanctuary in addition to two wildlife management units operated by the federal and provincial government. The park is also a popular location for winter sports such as ice fishing and skating.

(courtesy BC parks)

Additional Campgrounds

Cathedral

It is a great pity that access to this park involves a 25-kilometre gravel road and there are only 16 spots available for vehicle/tents as the park has a multitude of activities and spectacular scenery to offer. To reach the park, turn off Highway 3 three kilometres west of Keremeos and drive for 48 kilometres to the park entrance (as mentioned above, 25 kilometres are on gravel road). The park does provide a number of walk-in camping spots but no fresh water or firewood. The two main attractions on offer are fishing for rainbow and cutthroat trout and hiking a number of trails which facilitate appreciation of BC's back country and some excellent scenery. A private lodge operates in the park and provides four-wheel-drive transportation to the remoter hiking starting points. BC Parks produces a detailed leaflet describing all aspects of Cathedral Provincial Park that is a must for anyone planning to visit.

Dark Lake

With just five camping spots, picnic tables, two pit toilets but no fresh water nor wood, this campground nestled in a pine and fir forest is found by turning off Highway 97 at Summerland and traveling 20 kilometres northwest on a gravel road. Recreational pursuits are confined to fishing, canoeing, and hiking. Nearby Eneas Lakes Provincial Park also provides wilderness camping and hiking around four remote lakes.

Johnstone Creek

Not far from the intersection of Route 3 and Highway 33 is a small (38-hectare) functional campground with spaces for 16 vehicles/tents. There is no water, toilet facilities, nor picnic tables, but firewood is provided. Information from BC Parks records no recreational pursuits. The campground is, however, very near to Kettle River.

Pennask Lake

Located 55 kilometres northwest of Peachland and reached by turning off Highway 97C and taking a rough road for 50 kilometres, this campground has 28 spots, pit toilets, and picnic tables but no fresh water or firewood. The approach road is slow, bumpy, and regularly used by logging trucks, but it is accessible with a two-wheel-drive in the summer. Recreational activities include fishing and canoeing.

4   Kootenay Country

The comparatively quiet, undeveloped Kootenay region is one of the most scenic parts of the province and contains three mountain ranges: the Purcells, the Selkirks, and the Monashees. The area is home to fertile valleys, grasslands, huge lakes, and clear fresh rivers; yet it is an area devoid of any high concentration of population. Touring the Kootenays is a worry-free pleasure; on many occasions drivers find they have the road to themselves and it is easy to spot the abundant wildlife. Eleven provincial park campgrounds located on Highway 3 from Greenwood to Castlegar, on Highway 3A, Highway 31, and Highway 6 provide opportunities to experience this stunningly beautiful region and supply the ideal environment to get away from it all. Kootenay country is my favourite area of BC.

In addition to fine parks, the Kootenay region has a host of appealing communities. Nelson is the home to 350 heritage buildings including the City Hall.

Boundary Creek

Location
If you are debating whether to spend the night at Boundary Creek or another location my advice would be to choose the alternative. Conveniently situated on the banks of Boundary Creek three kilometres west of Greenwood, where all services are found, this two-hectare roadside campground has little to commend it.

Facilities
The 18 camping spots are quite large but the lack of dense vegetation makes them open and means there is little privacy. The campsites adjacent to the creek are somewhat more private as cottonwood trees line the banks of the creek itself. All the basic facilities offered by BC Parks are available (picnic tables, pit toilets, water, wood, fire pit). As the campground is close to the main road, it can be quite noisy.

Recreational activities
This is very much an overnight campground and therefore offers little recreational activity. It is possible to catch rainbow and brook trout in the creek. The mining industry developed the area adjacent to the campground. A nearby slag heap and crumbling stack are evidence of the BC Copper Company's smelter that employed over 400 men during its years of operation in the first part of the twentieth century. The historic town of Greenwood contains some beautiful turn-of-the-century buildings, including a court house and post office, and is a pleasant place to stroll around.

Additional information
Out of necessity I stayed at Boundary Creek in late September one year. The proximity to the road coupled with the openness of the sites themselves marks this as one of BC Parks' less desirable spots; however, it does have the advantage of being the only campground in the immediate area. I had visited

Greenwood during the late afternoon and had enjoyed it, so I went back in the evening, only to find it extremely quiet. Despite its claim to be Canada's smallest city, in Greenwood little occurs after 6:00 p.m.

But Greenwood does have a charming City Hall.
(courtesy The BC Adventure Network)

Champion Lakes

Location

The true Kootenay experience can be tasted at this provincial park. Situated in the Selkirk Mountains east of Trail at an elevation of 1,067 metres are a chain of three lakes which make up Champion Lakes. The park is 18 kilometres northwest of Fruitvale and is reached by turning off Highway 3 and taking a paved road. Services are present at Fruitvale and at Trail, half an hour's drive away.

Facilities

The facilities at this 95-spot campsite include a sani-station, flush and pit toilets, and a large day-use area. The campground itself is located between Second and Third Champion Lakes with trails leading to the waters. All spots are large, shady, and private, set in a forest of Douglas-fir, pine, and spruce. There is no wheelchair access. Reservations are accepted.

Recreational activities

Described as a canoeist's dream, this campground supplies a ribbon of lakes and portages and offers brilliant paddling potential. Development is concentrated around Third Champion Lake, which has a boat launch, playground, picnic area, and change house. Second and First Lakes remain in their natural states. Powerboats are prohibited. Swimming is a popular pastime here as is angling for rainbow and cutthroat trout. A number of hiking and walking trails lead from the campground, and interpretive programs are available in the summer.

Additional information

These lakes are named after James W. Champion, who was an early settler and orchardist in the area. First Champion Lake is about 1,500 metres long, with Second and Third being about 800 metres each. The park's location between the Coastal and Dry Biotic zones results in a diversity of plant species as well as more unusual animals such as beaver, porcupine, mink, and muskrat. If canoeing is your passion you should definitely include Champion Lakes on your list of prime paddling locations.

Gladstone/Texas Creek

Location

Residents of Christina Lake boast the waters are the warmest in BC. There is, however, debate over this claim as Wasa Lake and Osoyoos Lake also advance the same assertion. Whatever the truth, Christina Lake, an immensely popular recreational place where all services can be found, is home to Gladstone (formally named Texas Creek) Provincial Park. Gladstone is found just east of the community of Christina Lake off Highway 3, by turning onto East Lake Drive and driving for six kilometres on a paved road.

Facilities

Forty-eight camping spots are set in an open pine forest in the 112-hectare provincial park. The facilities include all the basic ones usually found (fire pit, water, picnic table, wood, pit toilets). In addition, Gladstone is wheelchair accessible.

Recreational activities

Nineteen kilometres long and only 55 metres deep, Christina Lake supplies a wealth of leisure pursuits including swimming from delightful secluded pocket beaches and boating and fishing in the clear waters. There is a hiking trail which leads north along the lakeshore. The nearby popular holiday centre also has golf courses and country clubs to enjoy.

Additional information

I have not had the opportunity to stay at Gladstone, but whenever I have driven through the Christina Lake area I have been amazed at its popularity. As I tend to want to avoid people and "commercialized" camping, the proximity of this provincial park to Christina Lake has tended to put me off. The resident population of 1,100 swells to over 6,000 at the height of summer as visitors come to enjoy the scenery and warm waters. While this popularity ensures all amenities are readily at hand, those who prefer more seclusion may find Gladstone a bit too busy.

(courtesy The BC Adventure Network)

Kokanee Creek

Location
It is difficult to imagine anyone not enjoying a visit to Kokanee Creek, situated among the beautiful scenery of the Slocan Range of the Selkirk Mountains. On the west arm of Kootenay Lake, 19 kilometres east of Nelson on Highway 3, this popular provincial park has a wealth of activities to offer all ages. Services are conveniently located in Nelson or Balfour (12 kilometres away).

Facilities
Kokanee Creek provides 132 wooded camping spots in two locations, Sandspit (numbers 1-113) and Redfish (114-132). Redfish is closer to the road, making Sandspit my personal preference. The site is home to the West Kootenay Visitor Centre so the facilities here are good and include flush toilets, a sani-station, and access for the disabled. There are no showers. Reservations are accepted.

Recreational activities
Kokanee Creek is a campground in which it is easy to spend a week. There are a wealth of things to see and do both in the park itself and the immediate vicinity. Activities linked with the water include swimming from wide sandy beaches, boating, water-skiing and sail boarding. The fishing is supposed to be excellent for both rainbow trout and kokanee. The world's largest rainbow trout—4.5 kg (10 lbs)— was landed here. Dolly Varden, char, burbot, and whitefish are also regularly caught. The visitor centre contains exhibits of natural and human history, and there are interpretive programs and walks. The nearby town of Nelson boasts the largest concentration of heritage buildings in BC, while farther north on Highway 3, visitors can walk through caves at Ainsworth Hot Springs and relax in therapeutic mineral pools.

Additional information
The spawning channel and interpretive programs offered here make this a truly educational place to visit. The word "kokanee" means "red fish" in the Kootenay Indian language and is the name given to the landlocked salmon which spawn here in large numbers. When I stayed (late August) the spawning was at its peak, and the interpretive program provided all the background information to this fascinating process. At dusk, bald eagles and ospreys can be seen diving for salmon, and while it appears sad that a few of these fish who have come so far with the sole thought of spawning will meet their demise so close to their destination, the spectacle is straight from a *National Geographic* television program. The salmon, together with the many other activities and the beautiful location, make this provincial park well worth a visit.

Kootenay Lake

Location

This beautiful quiet campground is in the heart of Kootenay country, with little to distract the camper other than mountain scenery and bald eagles flying overhead. On the west side of Kootenay Lake, north of Kaslo on Highway 31, this campground consists of two sites that provide a quiet, sheltered recreational spot. Services can be found in Kaslo, a 20-minute drive south.

Facilities

Twenty-six campsites are available at two locations, Davis Creek (12) and Lost Ledge (14). Some of these are very close to the lake and award fantastic views of the Purcell Mountains. There is no sani-station, and facilities consist of the basic ones found in BC Parks (wood, pit toilets, water, fire pit, and picnic tables).

Recreational activities

Leisure pursuits include swimming, boating (there is a boat launch at Lost Ledge), and fishing for kokanee, Dolly Varden, and rainbow trout. In addition, the quaint town of Kaslo is well worth a visit. From Kaslo it is possible to hire canoes, kayaks, and bikes to explore the lake and surrounding area. To the south, Ainsworth Hot Springs provide a relaxing afternoon's activity in mineral hot waters.

Additional information

This campground is located on a very quiet section of Highway 31. When I stayed, I cycled north to Duncan Dam then on to Howser, which has a small cafe. The highway follows the lake and has excellent views. There is another provincial park children and adults will adore located within easy access of Kootenay Lake. Cody Caves has no camping facilities and is situated in the Selkirk Mountains just above Ainsworth Hot Springs on 11 kilometres of good forest road off Highway 31. Visitors to this provincial park are treated to a full array of spectacular cave formations including stalagmites, stalactites, waterfalls, draperies, rimstone dams, and soda straws and must wear protective clothing and hard hats (the necessary equipment is provided) when taking the highly informative tours offered by BC Parks.

Visit the old Silver Ledge Hotel in Ainsworth which is now a museum. It contains many historic items like this cooking stove(on right).

Lockhart Beach

Location
This small, quaint, lakefront campground established in 1939 covers just three hectares and therefore is probably one of the smallest in the province. Lockhart Beach Provincial Park can be found on the east side of the South Arm of Kootenay Lake, 19 kilometres south of Kootenay Bay/Crawford. Food and lodging is available at Crawford Bay; more comprehensive services are located at Creston, an hour's drive south.

Facilities
The campground, primarily for overnight stops, has 13 camping spots with varying views of the lake. Facilities are restricted to the basic ones found in BC Parks (wood, pit toilets, water, fire pit, and picnic tables). There is no sani-station or access for the disabled.

Recreational activities
The park has a beach area from which it is possible to swim or to fish for rainbow trout and Dolly Varden. A trail leads from the park through a forest of Douglas-fir, redcedar, and ponderosa pine along Lockhart Creek, in which rainbow trout can be caught.

Additional information
Highway 3A from Creston to Kootenay Bay is a lovely drive and takes tourists past small stores, galleries, and the most amazing circular glass house constructed by a retired funeral director from 500,000 square embalming fluid bottles. Definitely the only one in Canada, if not the world, the house is found seven kilometres south of the campground. At Kootenay Bay, travellers can take the Kootenay Lake Ferry—the world's longest free ferry ride—across the lake to Balfour. When I took this trip there was an excellent little cafe on board, so make sure you embark hungry. This trip awards excellent photographic opportunities and should be taken by everyone holidaying in the area.

These photos are reproduced from Garnet Basque's *West Kootenay: The Pioneer Years.* This book and Elsie Turnbull's *Ghost Towns and Drowned Towns* provide intriguing reading for all Kootenay explorers.

McDonald Creek

Location

A perfect location for an evening's beach barbecue or lunchtime picnic awaits campers at McDonald Creek. Ten kilometres south of Nakusp, where all services can be found, this 468-hectare park occupies land on both the eastern and western shores of Upper Arrow Lake. Camping facilities are situated adjacent to the highway on the eastern side of the lake.

Facilities

Twenty-eight relatively private campsites are available in a lightly forested area; some overlook the lake. Facilities are confined to the basic ones found in BC Parks (wood, water, cooking pit, picnic tables, pit toilets).

Recreational activities

Massive Arrow Lake provides the central source of activity. From this location it is possible to fish for kokanee, Dolly Varden, and rainbow trout; to swim; to sunbathe; and to sail. A boat launch is available in the park. The nearby town of Nakusp is renowned for its hot springs. Located 12 kilometres along a gravel road north of Nakusp, this recreational site set high in the Selkirk Mountains contains two pools, one at 38 degrees centigrade, the other at 41 degrees. The views from these outdoor pools on to the Selkirk Mountains are quite spectacular, and if you choose the right time you could have this facility all to yourself.

Additional information

Arrow Lake, like Kootenay Lake, holds some of the world's largest rainbow trout known as the Gerrard. When I stayed here I had to stay at the overspill site, but even so had a wonderful time cooking dinner on the lakeside with a hibachi and watching the sun go down. Although it was full, the campground did not appear crowded and it has a good ambiance. Like many other communities in the Kootenays the economy of Nakusp has been dependent on the logging industry since 1910, and notwithstanding some diversification, remains so today. Evidence of the logging industry is never far away from the traveller vacationing in the Kootenays.

Nancy Greene

Location

This lovely park is by all accounts just as popular in the winter as the summer. Named after Canada's world-famous Olympic skier Nancy Greene, who came from the Rossland-Trail area, the park is situated in the Rossland Range of the Monashee Mountains, 35 kilometres north of Rossland on Highway 3. The park itself and the adjacent recreational area (which has the same name) are nestled in the Monashee Mountains and contain the subalpine Nancy Greene Lake. Services can be found at either Rossland or Castlegar, both communities being about half an hour's drive from the campground.

Facilities

There are ten campsites at this location primarily geared to tenters and smaller recreational vehicles. Larger RVs are allowed to camp in the parking lot. All the basic facilities exist, (pit toilets, wood, picnic tables, water, fire pit). There is no sani-station nor access for the disabled.

Recreational activities

As mentioned above, the park contains a subalpine lake and a lovely beach area from which it is possible to swim, fish for rainbow trout, or sail (powerboats are not allowed). A self-guided nature trail leads around the lake, while the adjacent Nancy Greene recreational area offers over 20 kilometres of hiking trails. The area is very popular in the winter for both downhill and cross-country skiing.

Additional information

The picturesque town of Rossland has a history dating back to the turn of the century. More recently it has gained a reputation for mountain biking. Just outside Rossland is the Le Roi Gold Mine, where visitors are taken underground to become acquainted with the life and work of a hardrock miner. Between 1900 and 1916 the Le Roi mine produced 50 percent of BC's gold and swelled the population of Rossland to 7,000 before its demise in the 1920s.

(courtesy BC Parks)

Rosebery

Location

Rosebery campground is undoubtedly one of the better campgrounds dedicated primarily to one-night stops. The scenery at this location is lovely; from here visitors can stare across Slocan Lake to the triumphant Valhalla Range of mountains. The park itself is situated on Highway 6, six kilometres south of Rosebery between Nakusp and New Denver, where services are available.

Facilities

Campers can take their pick from 36 large, private, shady camping spots suitable for every type of recreational vehicle. Some overlook the creek and are better than others which are in closer proximity to the road (although at night the road is not tremendously busy). There is no sani-station nor access for the disabled, and the facilities are confined to the basic ones provided in BC Parks (wood, pit toilets, water, fire pit, and picnic tables).

Recreational activities

Wilson Creek runs through the park and has a short trail leading along its edge. Fishing for rainbow trout is possible, and by crossing the lake you can explore and hike Valhalla Park. For those who prefer, there are also a number of private golf courses in the area.

Additional information

Located directly across Slocan Lake from Rosebery Provincial Park is Valhalla Park. This is a region of dramatic and diverse wilderness that includes lakes, alpine meadows, and the impressive New Denver glacier. With limited road access it offers 50,000 hectares of beautiful, unspoiled land to explore. Observant sailors heading towards Valhalla can spot pictographs painted by the forefathers of the Arrowhead Indian Band on the western shoreline of Slocan Lake.

Watch for historic markers on roadsides throughout BC.

Syringa Creek

Location

This area is rich in wildlife, so keep your eyes peeled for black bear, deer, and bighorn sheep. I believe Syringa Creek Provincial Park is misnamed; it is not really on a creek but on the eastern side of Lower Arrow Lake below the Norns Range of the Columbia Mountains. The lake, on the Columbia River resulted from the construction of the Keenleyside Dam. The campground is reached by turning off Highway 3A just north of Castlegar and traveling 19 kilometres on a paved road. All services are available in Castlegar while a nearby marina and store offers more limited supplies.

Facilities

Sixty large, private spots are available in a forest of redcedar, western hemlock, and ponderosa pine. In addition to all the basic facilities found in BC parks, Syringa Creek has a sani-station, flush and pit toilets, and wheelchair access.

Recreational activities

Syringa Creek boasts a fantastic sandy beach from which to view the Columbia Mountains and Monashee Range. All forms of water activity are possible, including swimming, boating, water-skiing (the park provides the only public launch in the area), and fishing for Dolly Varden and rainbow trout. For those who prefer non-water-based pursuits, a number of trails lead from the park for walking and mountain biking. (The Yellow Pine Trail is a particularly pleasant 45-minute interpretive trail.) There is an adventure playground and BC staff offer interpretive programs in the summer.

Additional information

The park is named after the Syringa or mock orange, a regional, white-flowered shrub which blooms in early spring. Nearby Castlegar is rich in Doukhobor history; a heritage museum near the airport details this culture and is worth a visit. Although the paved road ends at the park, an unpaved road carries on to an area known as Deer Park where there is an attractive waterfall.

Additional Campgrounds

Goat Range (Gerrard)

Located at the southeastern end of Trout Lake on Highway 31, a good gravel road, is a small campground 32 kilometres south of Trout Lake City. There are five vehicle/tent spots and some wilderness/walk-in camping units. There are two pit toilets but no water nor firewood. The area produces some of the province's largest lake trout, known as Gerrard. One caught here weighed 23.7 kilograms (52 lbs)! This park, is also known as Gerrard and Trout Lake Provincial Park. When I stopped here the mosquitoes were the size of birds.

5   British Columbia Rockies

Just mentioning the famous Canadian Rockies conjures up images of high, snow-capped mountains, ice fields, glaciers, lakes, V-shaped valleys, and waterfalls. When you travel in this region you will not be disappointed—you will see all these splendid features of the landscape and more. The following chapter provides details of the national and provincial parks situated in the Rocky Mountain/East Kootenay area of British Columbia on Highways 1, 93/95, 95, and 3. There are few large campgrounds here; instead the accommodation tends to consist of under 100 camping spots, nestled in one of the most spectacular areas of the province.

Spectacular scenery awaits as you drive through the BC Rockies.

Dry Gulch

Location

If hot springs are your passion, you'll love Dry Gulch. This beautiful little campground is five kilometres south of Radium Hot Springs, at the foot of Redstreak Mountain amid steep-sided gullies eroded by glaciers. All amenities can be found at Radium Hot Springs, just a short drive away. A one-kilometre gravel road from Highway 93 leads to the campground.

Facilities

Dry Gulch Provincial Park consists of 26 campsites set in a lightly forested area of Douglas-fir and ponderosa pine. All sites are large, private, and able to handle every type of recreational vehicle. There are flush and pit toilets but no sani-station or showers. The park is wheelchair accessible.

Recreational activities

One of the biggest attractions of staying here is the world-famous Radium Hot Springs, which are located in Kootenay National Park. Although they had been used by Interior and Plains native people for hundreds of years previously, the springs were formally established in 1911 and provide therapeutic waters to tourists and locals. The resort has a cafe, shop, and of course the relaxing mineral pools. Additional recreational activities in the vicinity include golf courses, Kootenay National Park, and the town of Radium. Watch for bighorn sheep, which are often observed on the grassland behind the campground.

Additional information

As this park is adjacent to Kootenay National Park, the campground is often used as an overspill location when the national park campgrounds are full. Kootenay National Park is situated on the west slope of the Continental Divide. It has over 200 kilometres of hiking trails and features alpine meadows, snow fields, lakes, and mountains (see page 94). Dry Gulch is an excellent quiet campground for enjoying the mineral waters.

Travelling in the Rockies watch for Rocky Mountain Bighorn Sheep. (courtesy Al Nickull)

Jimsmith Lake

Location
It is easy to see why this park is popular with both visitors and locals. Although it is relatively small (1.5 hectares), Jimsmith Lake is well situated at the western end of the Rocky Mountain Trench and surrounded by a forest of Douglas-fir, spruce, western larch, aspen, and lodgepole and ponderosa pine. The campground is located four kilometres south of Cranbrook on Highway 93/95. All services are available in Cranbrook.

Facilities
Twenty-eight large, private, well-spaced campsites suitable for every type of vehicle are available here. There is no sani-station. The park is wheelchair accessible and contains all basic amenities (water, wood, fire pit, picnic tables, pit toilets).

Recreational activities
Leisure pursuits include a developed swimming beach, canoeing and kayaking (powerboats are not allowed), and fishing for rainbow trout and large-mouthed bass. The park is frequently used for picnics and day trips by locals who relish the tranquillity it offers. The nearby town of Cranbrook houses the Canadian Museum of Rail Travel, where trains from an earlier era are shown and tea can be taken. Cranbrook also boasts a self-guided heritage tour on which you can see buildings that date from 1898 to 1929. Sixteen kilometres from Cranbrook is the heritage town of Fort Steele, where over 60 buildings from the turn of the century have been restored to recreate a bygone era.

Additional activities
This 12-hectare park is a popular location in winter for ice fishing, ice skating, Nordic skiing, sledding, and tobogganing. The economy of Cranbrook has been built on mining, fishing, and the railway. It is the largest town in the region (population 16,000) and has five provincial parks all within 30 minutes' drive.

Kikomun Creek

Location
Sometimes man's influence on the geography of an area is beneficial, as can be seen at Kikomun Creek Provincial Park. In the southern part of the Rocky Mountain Trench by Lake Koocanusa, this man-made lake was created by the construction of Libby Dam on the Kootenay River in Montana. The park has been enjoyed by campers since 1972. It can be reached by turning off Highway 3 at Jaffray and travelling 11 kilometres south on a paved road. Jaffray has limited services.

Facilities
Kikomun Creek, an ideal spot for family camping, provides a comprehensive range of facilities. Located in three campgrounds are 104 sites that can accommodate every type of recreational vehicle, a sani-station, flush and pit toilets, showers, and wheelchair access. Reservations can be made in the Surveyors' campground, which is where the showers are found.

Recreational activities
Fishing in this park is varied and good. The smaller lakes, (Hidden Lake and Surveyors' Lake) provide fishing potential for bass, eastern brook, rainbow trout, and Dolly Varden, while the 144-kilometre Koocanusa Reservoir has cutthroat trout and Rocky Mountain whitefish. Powerboats are not permitted on the smaller lakes, thus ensuring a peaceful time. There are two beaches, and picnic areas are found at Surveyors' Lake. Hiking trails around the smaller lakes offer opportunities to see elk, deer, badger, and ospreys. Old roads and railway beds give hikers and bikers easy access to the 682-hectare park. For young campers, there is an adventure playground in addition to a number of programs hosted by BC Parks during the summer.

Additional information
Kikomun Creek Provincial Park houses one of the largest collections of Western Painted Turtles, so-called because of the bright pattern underneath their shell. The turtles can easily be seen soaking up the sun. Kikomun Creek is a beautiful and varied place, ideal for a family vacation.

Watch for the
Western Painted Turtle

Kootenay National

Location

Along with Banff, Yoho, and Jasper, Kootenay National Park was designated a World Heritage Site in 1985 when UNESCO officially recognized the beauty and significance of the Rocky Mountain landscape. The only national park to contain both glaciers and cactus, Kootenay National Park is found on Highway 93 one kilometre north of Radium Hot springs (west park entrance) and straggles over 90 kilometres of the highway as it heads north. Services are located in Radium.

Facilities

In addition to back-country camping there are three locations for vehicle/ tent camping. Redstreak campground (my preference, where reservations are accepted) is just one kilometre from Radium Hot Springs and is a popular spot from which to gain access to the pools (a 30-minute trail leads from the campground to the waters). Redstreak has 242 spots set in a lightly forested area, showers, flush toilets, and a sani-station. Marble Canyon campground has 61 spots and is 86 kilometres north of Radium near the park's information centre. Set in a dense sub-alpine forest, Marble Canyon is the quietest of the three campgrounds. Mcleod River has 98 shady spots—some close to the water's edge, some quite small—26 kilometres north of Radium between Meadow Creek and Kootenay River. These two smaller campgrounds have only the basic facilities (pit toilets, water, wood, picnic tables, fire pit). A small charge ($3.00 in 1996) is made for firewood in all national parks.

Recreational activities

One of the biggest attractions here is of course the hot springs, valued for centuries for their rich healing powers and within easy access of Redstreak campground. The park has a number of hiking trails covering over 200 kilometres in addition to self guided trails. One of the more impressive shorter walks is Marble Canyon, a 30-minute trail that takes visitors into an ice-carved limestone and dolomite canyon with interpretive boards detailing its 500-million-year development. Other recreational pursuits include horseback riding, mountaineering, canoeing and rafting down the Kootenay River, swimming, and wildlife viewing. While it is possible to fish for brook and rainbow trout, most of the streams and rivers are glacier-fed, so the waters are too cold to yield high fish populations.

Additional information

As in all national parks, visitor permits are required by all who plan to stop. These are available at the park entrance and can be used in any Canadian national park. An attendant told me that Kootenay National Park is often overlooked. There are hundreds of things to do here, and wildlife (moose, black bear, elk, deer, and over 179 species of birds) does appear to be more readily observable. The Banff-Windermere Highway which runs through the park was built in 1922 and was the first road constructed through the Canadian Rockies. It is a very pleasant drive from which to spot animal life.

Mount Fernie

Location

Rich in native legend of unrequited love, broken promises, and catastrophes, this 259-hectare park in the shadow of Mount Fernie has been described as the eastern gateway to the Kootenays. It is located three kilometres west of the settlement of Fernie on Highway 3. Services are provided at Fernie.

Facilities

The campground has 38 campsites set amongst a parkland of diverse vegetation including western larch, Douglas-fir, black cottonwood, trembling aspen, western redcedar, and spruce. There are flush and pit toilets but no sani-station or showers. The park is not wheelchair accessible.

Recreational activities

The main attraction of this park is a three-kilometre interpretive trail which winds its way through the park and takes visitors to picturesque Lizard Creek and waterfalls. The walk from the park's parking lot to the falls also makes a pleasant break for those who are not intending to spend the night here. The park has areas of old-growth forest and wildlife viewing opportunities for black bears, elk, and deer which are commonly found. The town of Fernie, just three kilometres from the park, has a historical museum, buildings dating back to 1904, and a historical walking tour as well as a cultural centre and restaurant on the site of the former Canadian Pacific Railway station.

Additional information

Fernie is named after William Fernie, who was instrumental in the development of coal mining in the area. Legend tells that William Fernie found out about the coal deposits from the Tobacco Plains People by promising to marry one of their young women. After gaining this information he rejected her, thereby provoking her father to place a curse on the name "Fernie." The town did suffer calamity in the form of a mine explosion that killed 128 men in 1902; two fires in 1904 and 1908, the latter leaving 6,000 people homeless; and floods. In 1964 Chief Red Eagle of the Tobacco Plains Band lifted the curse. Some people still believe that on summer nights the ghost of an Indian princess led by her father rides across Hosmer Mountain in a search for William Fernie. So when you stay here, be on the lookout for this apparition.

Moyie Lake

Location

A restful, relaxing time awaits the camper at this beautiful provincial park. Adjacent to the eastern fringe of the Purcell Mountains near the northern end of Moyie Lake is a campground that supplies a beautiful retreat, especially for those with young children. Its excellent location is 20 kilometres south of Cranbrook (where all services are available), and ten kilometres north of Moyie.

Facilities

A comprehensive range of facilities exists at this ground, which accommodates 104 camping spots. The park has full disabled access, a sani-station, flush toilets, and showers. The campsites themselves are all large and private. Reservations are accepted. The only disadvantage is that a railroad operates quite near to the campground and may cause problems for light sleepers.

Recreational activities

A wealth of activities can be enjoyed at Moyie Lake. Campers can take the two-kilometre Meadow Interpretive Trail, which describes the forest typical to the area. Swimming is easy from a protected swimming area, and for fishermen, the lake contains Dolly Varden (up to 1.5 kg), kokanee (to 30 cm), rainbow trout (to 1.5 kg), and eastern brook trout (to 1 kg). A boat launch is available and windsurfing is possible, weather permitting. For children there is an adventure playground, and interpretive programs throughout the summer keep the whole family entertained.

Additional information

This park is an ideal location to spend time in if you have a young family, but it is not just for those with children. For campers who decide not to cook over an open fire, the pub situated about ten minutes south of the campground on Highway 3 is worth a visit, while the nearby town of Cranbrook supplies all services should you have forgotten one of the basic camping needs. Moyie Lake is a delightful location to set up camp. When I stayed, the only drawback was the three jet-skiers who shattered the calm of the afternoon and made me appreciate the lakes on which powerboats are prohibited.

Norbury Lake

Location
Norbury Lake is nestled in the Hughes Range of the Rocky Mountains and supplies excellent views of the Steeples—a distinctive feature of the Hughes Range and also of the Purcell Mountains. The park is easily found 13 kilometres southwest of Fort Steele on a paved road from Highway 93/95. Services are available at Fort Steele.

Facilities
This is a secluded location for 46 camping spots set amongst Douglas-fir, lodgepole pine, ponderosa pine, and western larch. There is no sani-station nor disabled access, and facilities are restricted to the basic ones found in BC parks (water, wood, fire pit, picnic tables, pit toilets).

Recreational activities
Recreational pursuits within the park include fishing for rainbow trout in Peckhams Lake, swimming, and boating (powerboats are prohibited). Two trails are available to lead explorers over a diverse area of lightly forested landscape where it is possible to see elk, deer, and Rocky Mountain Bighorn sheep. Norbury Lake is close to the historic town of Fort Steele, a fascinating example of turn-of-the-century life in Canada and a real delight to visit. In 1961 the provincial government recognized Fort Steele as being of historical significance, and the reconstruction which started then continues today. A perfect example of a pioneer town, Fort Steele contains some 50 buildings, including an original North West Mounted Police camp, excellent bakery, restaurant, theatre and museum.

Additional information
Norbury Lake is named after F. Paget Norbury, a magistrate who served in Fort Steele in the late nineteenth century. This park is the site of the Kootenai Indian ceremonial grounds. An informative display giving details of their culture is found at Peckhams Lake entrance.

Premier Lake

Location

Long before the time of BC Parks, the K'tunaxa aboriginal people used this area for camping, hunting, and fishing. Today, campers are attracted to the region for the splendid views. In the Hughes Range of the Rockies about 45 kilometres northeast of Kimberley is Premier Lake. It is reached by turning off Highway 95 at Skookumchuk (a Chinook word meaning "strong or turbulent water") and travelling 16 kilometres on a gravel road. (Watch for logging trucks which frequently travel at speed along this route.) A gas station, shop, and restaurant are available at Skookumchuk.

Facilities

Set amongst a mixed vegetation of Douglas-fir, western larch, cottonwood, and aspen are 56 campsites. Facilities are confined to the basic ones found in BC Parks (water, wood, fire pit, picnic tables, pit toilets). The park is wheelchair accessible. An unusual manually operated solar-heated shower is available at this location.

Recreational activities

Five lakes—Premier, Canuck, Yankee, Cats Eyes, and Quart—exist in this 662-hectare park that has gained a reputation as a good spot to fish for eastern brook trout and Gerrard rainbow trout. A short walk from the campground there is a spawning and viewing area together with an interpretive display to explain enhancement procedures, including how eggs are collected for the Kootenay Trout Hatchery. There is a boat launch and swimming is available. The park also contains a number of trails that cover a variety of distances and take between 20 minutes and two hours to complete. For children, an adventure playground is found at the entrance to the campground.

Additional information

To respect the archaeological significance of the area, facilities in the park have been built above ground. The area is rich in wildlife—watch for elk roaming on the cleared hills near the highway. Premier Lake is yet another BC provincial park located in spectacular, breathtaking scenery.

Wasa Lake

Location

This gem of a campground is one of the largest in the region and provides a comprehensive range of facilities and activities. The campground lies on the northern end of Wasa Lake, a glacier-formed kettle lake, reputed to be one of the warmest in the east Kootenays if not the province. (Osoyoos and Christina both also claim this distinction.) The views from the Wasa Lake campground are staggering, with the Rocky Mountains to the east and the Purcells to the west. Wasa Lake Provincial Park is situated 40 kilometres north of Cranbrook on Highway 93/95. The community of Wasa, one kilometre away, has stores, a gas station, restaurants, laundry facilities, and a neighbourhood pub.

Facilities

This campground can accommodate every type of recreational vehicle in 104 well-appointed camping spots set among pine and aspen trees. There are flush and pit toilets and a sani-station but no showers. The campground is wheelchair accessible and reservations are accepted.

Recreational activities

The lake supplies a wealth of recreational activities with four excellent beaches giving access to warm waters. There is a boat launch and fishing for large-mouthed bass is a favourite pursuit. A self-guided nature trail that takes about an hour (two kilometres) gives details of the flora and fauna of the area. A 33-kilometre mountain-bike trail leads from Wasa Lake to Lazy Lake, (BC Parks has published a leaflet describing the details of this trail), and there is also an adventure playground. The park has an amphitheatre with a regular schedule of programs throughout the summer. In addition to the recreational activities provided in the park itself, the historic town of Fort Steele is only 18 kilometres to the south; likewise, the Bavarian community of Kimberley, Canada's highest city, is within easy reach. Here visitors can marvel at the world's largest operating cuckoo clock, stop at gingerbread-fronted stores, or play a round of golf.

Additional information

Each year on the Sunday of the August long weekend a sand sculpture contest is held on Camper's Beach, the main beach on the lake. The park contains a variety of vegetation including an area of endangered grasslands.

Whiteswan Lake

Location

Driving to Whiteswan Lake can be an adventure in itself. The gravel road is frequented by huge logging trucks and in places narrows to one lane, necessitating excellent driving skills. The journey is well worth the effort. This provincial park is located on a plateau in the Kootenay Range of the Rocky Mountains east of Canal Flats, where limited services are available. Both Alces and Whiteswan lakes are contained in the almost 2,000-hectare park, which has some fantastic views of the surrounding mountains. The campground is reached by turning off Highway 93/95 and travelling along Whiteswan Lake Road (gravel) for 18 kilometres.

Facilities

The park has four campgrounds, providing 88 spaces in total. Alces Lake has a sani-station and is reached after travelling 21 kilometres from the main highway. Packrat Point is at kilometre 24, Inlet Creek a further four kilometres along the road, and Home Basin is the most distant. Home Basin and Alces Lake have lakeside camping. There are also wilderness campsites in the park. In addition to all the basic amenities (water, wood, fire pit, picnic tables, pit toilets) the park is wheelchair accessible.

Recreational activities

One of the main attractions of this location is the undeveloped Lussier Hot Springs, near the park's western boundary. The hot springs flow from the mountainside into a series of pools, and, unlike the ones at Radium, Ainsworth, or Fairmont, are unspoiled by commercial development. Both Whiteswan and Alces Lakes provide plenty of swimming opportunities with a beach at the north end of Whiteswan Lake. The two lakes are among the most productive fisheries in the East Kootenays, and in May and June rainbow trout can be seen spawning in Inlet and Outlet Creeks. Boat launches are available at Packrat Point and Home Basin (electric motors only on Alces Lake). An eight-kilometre hiking trail takes walkers from Alces Lake to Home Basin, and there are opportunities for viewing wildlife such as golden eagles, bald eagles, mountain goats, bighorn sheep, and moose. ("Alces" is Latin for "moose".)

Additional information

This is an area rich in history. It has been used by the K'tunaxa (Kootenai) native people for over 5,000 years. In the 1800s and 1900s trappers and prospectors worked the region, while today logging is the prime industry— a fact you will be well aware of if you encounter a logging truck on your journey to this beautiful away-from-it-all camping location.

Yahk

Location

This nine-hectare park can be found in a quiet, uncommercialized area of BC, on the banks of the Moyie River. It is close to the United States border and the state of Idaho. Situated on Highway 39 at Yahk, 39 kilometres east of Creston, Yahk Provincial Park is very much an overnight camping or picnic spot. Services can be found in Moyie, Yahk, or Creston.

Facilities

There are 24 campsites here set amidst a forest of Douglas-fir, lodgepole pine, and ponderosa pine. The facilities are confined to the basic ones found in BC Parks (firewood, cooking pit, picnic table, water, pit toilets). The park is located close to both the railway line and road, so the noise of traffic may be disturbing to some.

Recreational activities

Yahk is primarily for one-night campers or for brief rest stops, and there is not a great deal to do here besides fish in the Moyie River for Dolly Varden. As you travel down Highway 3/95 following the Moyie River, moose and mule deer can be seen feeding, so keep your eyes peeled.

Additional information

Yahk was once a major supplier for railway ties to the Canadian Pacific Railway, an industry that still exists but has been in steady decline since the 1940s. Today, Yahk has a population of almost 200. Set on a hillside overlooking the lake, the pretty community of Moyie to the south has some interesting buildings. Moyie owes its development to lead-silver mining, and at one time was the richest mine of this type in the province.

(courtesy of BC Parks)

Yoho National

Location

"Yoho" is thought to be the word used by the Kootenai people to express awe, and visitors certainly have this emotion in Yoho, Canada's second oldest national park. Designated by UNESCO as a World Heritage Site and often compared to the Swiss Alps, Yoho has spectacular lakes, mountains, ice fields, alpine meadows, glaciers, and waterfalls. Found on the Trans-Canada Highway between Golden and Lake Louise, the small community of Field in the park has services.

Spectacular scenery is yours to enjoy. (courtesy Al Nickull)

Facilities

Over 300 camping spots are available from which campers can access the delights of Yoho. The three main vehicle/tent campgrounds are Kicking Horse, in a lightly forested area five kilometres east of Field (86 spots), Chancellor Peak, five kilometres from the western park boundary (64 spots), and Hoodoo Creek, seven kilometres from the western boundary (106 spots). Showers, flush toilets, and a sani-station are available at Kicking Horse, which also has overflow camping, an outdoor interpretive theatre and a play area for children. Hoodoo is densely wooded and peaceful; it has flush toilets and a sani-station but no showers. Chancellor Peak provides only the basic camping facilities but has great views and is on the Kicking Horse River. In addition, walk-in campsites a short distance from the car park are available at Takakkaw Falls (35 spots). Monarch, with 46 spots, is the most recent addition. A number of primitive camping facilities also exist in the park. Park-use permits are required for overnight camping, and in 1996 a $3.00 charge was made for firewood.

Recreational activities

Visitors to Yoho should make their first port of call the Yoho Park Information Centre located at the junction of Highway 1 and Field. From here, detailed maps of the vicinity can be obtained. In a park of this size (131,300 hectares), internationally recognized for its beauty, there is a multitude of things to do, including canoeing (canoes can be rented on Emerald Lake), rafting, fishing, mountain biking, mountaineering, and of course, hiking. Fantastic hiking opportunities abound, with visitors able to choose between short interpretive trails and hikes that last for days. When I stayed, I hiked the Iceline Trail, which takes you to glaciers, alpine meadows, forests, and mountains among

Takakkaw Fall is spectacular.
(courtesy Al Nickull)

some of the best scenery in the world. It is impossible to recommend this trail too highly. The Iceline trail (and others) has views of the Takakkaw Falls, at 254 metres one of the highest waterfalls in North America. "Takakkaw" is a Cree word meaning "magnificent."

Additional information

Yoho National Park was established in 1911. Yoho owes its development to the Canadian National Railway workers who managed to push the tracks through Kicking Horse Pass and build the first company hotel in Field. Climbers, tourists, and artists came to the hotel and recognized the overpowering beauty of the area. In 1886 Mount Steven Reserve was set aside, and in 1911 it was renamed Yoho.

Additional Campgrounds

Bugaboo

This is an alpine wilderness park containing the largest glaciers in the Purcells. It is found by turning off Highway 95, 27 kilometres north of Radium Hot Springs, then taking a good gravel road for 45 kilometres. Wilderness/walk-in camping spots are available in addition to camping huts. There are four pit toilets and fresh water. The main attractions here are the hiking trails which lace across the terrain; many should be undertaken only by those with experience. Climbing is also a popular activity, and there is a commercial lodge in the park which provides heli-skiing and heli-hiking in remote areas of the park.

6   High Country

This diverse region stretching from the eastern side of BC to the middle of the province incorporates three of the most spectacular provincial parks: Mount Robson is named after its majestic mountain, the highest in the Canadian Rockies; Wells Gray is BC's fourth largest park and known as "the waterfall park"; and Shuswap Lake is a recreational paradise with over 1,000 kilometres of waterways and numerous sandy beaches. With scenery ranging from the Rocky Mountains in the east to grasslands in the west, the area has something for everyone. This chapter includes national and provincial park campgrounds located on a section of Highway 16, from the border of Alberta to Route 5, Highway 5 as far south as Merritt, Highway 5A to Aspen Grove, Route 1 as far as Lytton, and the north section of Highway 23.

Mount Robson Provincial Park in all its glory.

Adams Lake

Location

Visitors to Adams Lake discover a paradise of pristine beaches covering over 2,500 metres of shoreline. The campground is beautifully situated near the warm southern end of the 60-kilometre-long lake. It is found by turning off Highway 1 at Squilax and taking a paved road which turns into a gravel road for 15 kilometres. The park is 30 kilometres from Chase, which houses the nearest services.

Facilities

The small, lightly forested campground has 32 spots. Facilities are restricted to the basic ones found in BC parks (pit toilets, wood, water, picnic tables, fire pit).

Recreational activities

Caves nestle along the shore, and all types of water sports can be enjoyed, including swimming, boating, sunbathing, fishing, windsurfing, and paddling. Many visitors simply enjoy relaxing in this remote location. The campground is located 15 kilometres north of Roderick Haig-Brown Provincial Park, dedicated to preserving one of BC's primary natural resources and site of the largest sockeye salmon run on the continent. Every four years, millions of sockeye return here. In the intervening years the runs are smaller but still significant. Trails allow riverside access to this amazing phenomenona.

Additional information

Adams Lake Provincial Park was established in 1988 and is a relatively recent addition to BC Parks. The park, which incorporates an area of 56 hectares, offers an idyllic spot for those who seek a tranquil location yet one which is easily accessible from Route 1.

Arrow Lakes/Shelter Bay

Location

Take the camera and marvel at the sunsets from this quaint little roadside campground. Located on the western side of Upper Arrow Lake and found by travelling 50 kilometres south of Revelstoke on Highway 23, it is near the ferry crossing for Gatena Bay. The nearest services are at Revelstoke.

Facilities

Thirteen camping spots are available. They are positioned quite close together and as there is no vegetation they afford little privacy. Some do, however, overlook the lake; these spots provide beautiful views of the water and the landscape beyond. All the basic amenities found in BC Parks are available (pit toilets, picnic tables, water, wood, fire pits), and those who prefer flush toilets and sinks can find them a short walk away at Shelter Bay.

Recreational activities

This campground is primarily for overnighters. The lake is excellent to swim in, and fishing for rainbow trout, Dolly Varden, and kokanee is possible. There is also a boat launch.

Additional information

Even though the campground is meant primarily for overnighters, the park is a pleasant place to stop because of its proximity to the lake and to the views of the rugged Selkirk Mountains that reach over 3,000 metres. Although the campground is near the road, traffic ceases at 9:30 p.m. when the ferries stop, so the location is very peaceful during darkness. The ferry ride from Shelter Bay to Galena Bay is free and provides a beautiful break from driving to enjoy the scenery. I stayed here in August, and the campground was barely half full. With no traffic noise and a beautiful lake in which to bathe, this is definitely one of the better roadside camping spots.

Blanket Creek

Location
In its former life, Blanket Creek was a busy homestead, and today it is easy to see why the original pioneers chose to settle here. Created as a provincial park in 1982, this delightful 316-hectare park is located at the point where Blanket Creek enters the Columbia River, 25 kilometres south of Revelstoke on Highway 23. The nearest services are available at Revelstoke.

Facilities
Sixty-four well-positioned, large camping spots, set in a lightly forested area and all with spectacular views of the Monashee Mountains, are available here. There are flush and pit toilets but no sani-station or access for the disabled.

Recreational activities
In the day-use area of Blanket Creek a large beach-rimmed lagoon ideal for swimming has been constructed. A trail leads from the campground to the pool. A five-minute walk along the Old South Road takes campers to the beautiful 12-metre-high Sutherland Falls, and there is also a route suitable for bikes. Fishing in both the creek and Upper Arrow Lake can yield Dolly Varden, rainbow trout, and kokanee, and in the fall, kokanee can be seen spawning in the mouth of the creek. The nearby town of Revelstoke is a lovely place to visit. Revelstoke offers a golf course, railway museum, piano museum, and local history museum as well as a number of cobbled streets and turn-of-the-century buildings to explore.

Additional information
The site contains the remains of the Domke homestead, one of the few properties unaffected by the flooding of the Arrow Reservoir. The original log home dating back to the 1920s is still standing, while many of the other brick buildings were dismantled leaving only a pool and rock well with arched driveway. The land was abandoned in the late 1960s when the Hugh Keenleyside Dam near Castlegar and the flooding of Arrow Reservoir was completed. Blanket Creek supplies a pleasant, quiet camping experience.

Glacier National

Location

A region of spectacular high mountain scenery shaped by avalanches and snow, Glacier National Park is found in the Northern Selkirk Range of the Columbia Mountains 49 kilometres east of Revelstoke on Highway 1. The park is aptly named. Nearly 12 percent of its total 136,500-hectare area is comprised of over 400 active glaciers and ice fields. Services located adjacent to the Rogers Pass Information Centre in the park include a gas station, hotel, cafe, and shop.

Facilities

Three campgrounds offering over 300 spaces exist here. Mountain Creek campground, closest to the park's northeastern entrance, is in a heavily wooded area with 250 sites, flush toilets but no showers. Of the three, this is the easiest campground in which to find accommodation. Loop Brook has 20 spots and is located 14 kilometres from the western entrance; Illecillewaet, 17 kilometres from Loop Brook, has 59 spots. There is no sani-station and no showers, but flush toilets are available in these smaller campgrounds. As Glacier is a national park, a small fee is collected for firewood (in 1996 this was $3.00).

Recreational activities

Anyone visiting the park should stop at the visitor centre, which has displays of natural and human history as well as videos illustrating various aspects of the park, its early relationship with the railroad, and subsequent development. The centre, designed in the shape of a massive snow shed, is an attraction in itself. Park staff are always willing to provide advice on Glacier's numerous attractions and can gear suggestions to your own preferences and time scale. Twenty-one hiking trails zigzag across 140 kilometres and include the Abandoned Rails Interpretive Trail that starts at the information centre. Renowned for climbing and mountaineering opportunities, the park also offers potential for canoeing, horseback riding, and fishing for whitefish, Dolly Varden, and trout in the Illecillewaet River.

Additional information

Even if you do not intend to stay at Glacier, stop and visit the information centre and learn about the history of Rogers Pass. The pass was first discovered by railway engineer Major A.B. Rogers in 1882, and by 1885 railway construction had been completed. In 1956 the Trans-Canada Highway was routed through the area, and the road linking the Illecillewaet River on the west to the Beaver River on the east was completed in 1962. Videos and displays give testimony to how hazardous and challenging this construction process was. Today, experts constantly monitor the snow conditions, and there is an avalanche control program.

Goldpan

Location

Watch out for river rafters and gold prospectors if you plan to sojourn here. Goldpan is a five-hectare roadside provincial park conveniently located on Highway 1 ten kilometres south of Spences Bridge, where services are located.

Facilities

There are just 14 camping spots available here beside the mighty Thompson River. Facilities are confined to the basic ones found in BC Parks (wood, water, fire pit, picnic tables, pit toilets). Railway trucks and the noise of road traffic can be heard from the campground.

Recreational activities

Goldpan's main attraction is fishing, and the park attracts steelhead anglers, especially during the months of October, November, and December. In addition, the area is known for whitewater rafting, and often adventurers can be seen navigating the currents of the Thompson River in their rubber rafts. Consequently, the area is heavily used during the peak summer months by commercial river-rafting companies looking for a resting place for their down river trips. As one would surmise, gold panning is also a pursuit that can be undertaken here.

Additional information

Spences Bridge, named after Thomas Spence, who built the original bridge in 1865, is where the Thompson and Nicola Rivers meet. This area has been fished for hundreds of years by the Thompson Indian people, who continue to fish here today, as indeed do many others. For those who want a taste of adventure by whitewater rafting, this location is ideal. Be warned — in summertime the area is prone to some very high temperatures, often the highest in the country, so remember the sun screen.

(courtesy The BC Adventure Network)

109

Herald

Location

A variety of flora and fauna together with easy access to the calm waters of Shuswap Lake are just two of the many attributes of Herald Provincial Park. The vegetation is attributable to the park's distinctive position amongst steep uplands and flat deltas. It includes Douglas-fir, juniper, dry land shrubs, redcedar, hemlock, cottonwood, aspen, and paper birch. A naturalist's delight, Herald is found on the Salmon Arm of Shuswap Lake, 12 kilometres east of Tappen off Route 1. Services are available at Tappen.

Facilities

On the calm lakeside are 51 beautiful wooded camping spaces with all the services required for a comfortable camping experience, including showers, flush and pit toilets, a sani-station, and wheelchair access. Reservations are accepted.

Recreational activities

Shuswap Lake is a relatively warm lake and therefore a delightful place to swim. The park has sand and fine gravel beaches ideal for sunbathing. Fishing and boating are pursuits enjoyed by many, and there are a number of trails including one which leads through an area of cedar growth to the beautiful Margaret Falls. Reinecker Creek runs through the park near to the campground, and evidence of Indian pit houses is visible west of the creek.

Additional information

The lake is named after the Shuswap Indians, who recognized it as bountiful for hunting and fishing. Cliff faces around the lake display pictographs (rock paintings) that provide evidence of man's long inhabitation of the region. While the lake is named after the aboriginal people, the park takes its name from the Herald family, who were early settlers to the area. The remains of the family's farm buildings can still be seen today. Herald Provincial Park is very popular with both locals and tourists as it offers every facility yet is not tremendously large. It's a delightful place to camp.

Juniper Beach

Location

Juniper Beach is distinct from many other provincial parks you may stay in because of its dry desert setting. Established in 1989 and not yet ten years old, it is one of BC's newer parks. Juniper Beach is located 19 kilometres east of Cache Creek on Highway 1. Services are available at Cache Creek or Kamloops, 53 kilometres to the west.

Facilities

On the banks of the Thompson River 35 camping spots are yours for the taking. The vegetation is relative desert and consists of sagebush, prickly pear cactus, juniper, and cottonwoods. Although the camping spots accommodate every type of recreational vehicle, they are somewhat open. The campground is wheelchair accessible and has pit toilets, a sani-station and a shower. Located a fair distance from the road, the campsites are not affected by the noise of traffic, but the railway line is close by.

Recreational activities

This provincial park provides one of the few access places to the Thompson River between Savona and Spences Bridge and is excellent for steelhead and rainbow trout fishing. A large natural pool separated from the river is perfect for swimming, and canoeing and kayaking are also possible.

Additional information

This campground is located in the desert area of the Thompson-Nicola region and so looks quite barren compared to BC parks in more fertile regions. Do not expect to find much shade here on a hot summer day! The easy access down to the Thompson River makes Juniper Beach a pleasant place to stay, and picnics on the shoreline are a delight. Literature from BC Parks states this is a good place to view sockeye salmon and to witness the summer migration of Chinook and coho, although when I stayed there was no evidence of any fish either in the river or being caught by the patient anglers.

(courtesy The BC Adventure Network)

Kentucky-Alleyne

Location

Campers from the Lower Mainland looking for a weekend getaway cannot go wrong in choosing Kentucky-Alleyne, a real gem of a campground. Situated 38 kilometres south of Merritt, it is found by turning off Highway 5A and taking a three-kilometre gravel road. Services are available in Merritt.

Facilities

Sixty-three camping spots can be found in this park. While the units do not have the advantage of vegetation to afford privacy, they are well spaced and suitable for every type of recreational vehicle. Four camping spaces are set a kilometre away from the rest at the other end of the lake, while some spots are on the lakeside. Facilities are confined to the basic ones found in BC Parks (pit toilets, fire pit, picnic tables, wood, water).

Recreational activities

This is a stunningly beautiful area consisting of glacial undulating hills and grasslands surrounded by forests of pine and fir in the heart of cattle country. The many lakes offer fishing potential for rainbow trout (I love the way that one of the smaller lakes is restricted for "children only" fishing) and are annually stocked. Swimming is a delight here as is canoeing. A number of trails take visitors around the lakes to different areas of the park where it is possible to see beaver lodges. As the campground is spread out, cycling on the many gravel roads and trails makes an enjoyable pastime for all ages; there are, however, a number of private roads which display "no trespassing" signs.

Additional information

I love this park. While the camping spots themselves are not stunning, the size of the camping area and the many dirt trails and roads around the park, together with the glacial topography, make Kentucky-Alleyne a pleasant place to explore. The sunsets are gorgeous and it is magical to cook dinner on an open fire while watching the beautiful red sun set over the water as ospreys circle above. For those who want to avoid others and do not mind a bumpy road, the four detached camping spots at the far end of the lake make a good retreat into your own private campsite.

(courtesy BC Parks)

Lac Le Jeune

Location
If you are looking for a base from which to explore the region, this relatively small (47-hectare) lakeside provincial park, easily accessible from Kamloops and Merritt, is an excellent bet. It is situated 37 kilometres south of Kamloops on Highway 5 and 47 kilometres north of Merritt, with a full range of services being found at both locations.

Facilities
Set among a forest of pinegrass and lodgepole pines are 144 large, well-positioned campsites. A few of these spots have the added advantage of being close to the lake. A sani-station and flush toilets are in the day-use area. The park is wheelchair accessible.

Recreational activities
Lac Le Jeune is equipped with a boat launch, and swimming is possible in a protected swimming area. All the literature on the park states that the lake is famous for "fighting rainbow trout," so go win a battle! A trail leads from the day-use area to the Stake/McConnell trail systems in the adjacent Stake/McConnell Lake Recreational area. This area has 160 kilometres of trails for hiking and mountain biking during the summer and cross-country skiing in the winter. Interpretive programs are offered in the summer and there is an adventure playground. Walloper Lake Provincial Park, a short drive from here off Highway 5, only has wilderness camping but does offer canoe and boat rentals and therefore access to the beautiful waters of the area.

Additional information
During the hot dry days of summer this campground, which is at a higher elevation than Thompson Valley to the north and Nicola Valley in the south, provides much welcomed cooler climatic conditions. As mentioned above, Lac Le Jeune is an excellent base from which to explore the towns of Merritt, Kamloops, and Logan Lake.

Martha Creek

Location
The views from this campground which overlooks the Revelstoke Reservoir stretch on to the Monashee Mountain Range and provide fantastic photographic opportunities. For this reason alone, Martha Creek is a delightful place to sojourn. Martha Creek is situated 19 kilometres north of Revelstoke on Highway 23. All services are available at Revelstoke.

Facilities
Located on an old river terrace on the western shore of Revelstoke reservoir, Martha Creek has 25 well-spaced campsites, many with access directly onto the beach. There are flush and pit toilets but no sani-station. The park is not wheelchair accessible.

Recreational activities
A swimming beach is located near the campground, and a boat launch is found at the eastern boundary of the park. Fishing in the Revelstoke Reservoir includes kokanee, rainbow trout, and Dolly Varden. An enchanting seven-kilometre hiking trail leads walkers through wildflowers, cedar, and hemlock and on to flowering meadows and alpine lakes within the Sleeker Mountains. The historic town of Revelstoke has been restored over the last few years and supplies an attractive location for shopping and wandering. In the summertime the bandstand (or gazebo) in the town's plaza has evening entertainment for visitors. I spent a lovely August evening dancing to a local band as the sun went down—just the sort of light exercise needed before retiring to the tent or RV.

Additional information
If staying in the vicinity, you must visit the Revelstoke Dam, one of North America's largest and most modern hydroelectric developments, located five minutes from Revelstoke on the road to Martha Creek. Mica Dam, two hours north of Revelstoke on Highway 23, is also worth a visit. Both offer fascinating tours of their facilities and interesting programs on how and why they were constructed.

Monck

Location

With fantastic views of the Nicola Valley south of Kamloops and within easy reach of Merritt, the nearest large settlement, this campground has a great deal to offer. Monck Provincial Park is found by taking Highway 5A to Nicola, then a paved road to the campground situated 21 kilometres north of Merritt. All services are available in Merritt.

Facilities

With the exception of showers, this 71-space campground has all the necessary requirements for camping (including a sani-station, flush toilets, and access for the disabled). The cheery camping spots, set among a forest of ponderosa pine and fir on the north side of Nicola Lake, are suitable for every type of recreational vehicle.

Recreational activities

Monck Provincial Park is an ideal family vacation spot. There is a safe sandy beach leading to the beautiful waters of Nicola Lake. Fishing for kokanee is reputed to be excellent, and there is a concrete boat launch to facilitate boating and sailing pursuits. A number of trails lead from the campground through a forest to various vantage points. Indian pit house depressions can also be located here, and a walk along an old road to Second Beach leads to a fine example of Indian rock paintings (pictographs).

Additional information

The Nicola Valley is surrounded by green fields and rich marshland. Originally settled by ranchers, the area is now home to Canada's largest working cattle ranch, the Douglas Lake Ranch, offering horseback riding and ranch tours. The land which now includes Monck was donated by Major Charles Sidney Goldman in honour of his son, Lieutenant Commander "Pen" Monck, a British World War Two soldier who changed his name to Monck to improve his chances of survival should he be captured by the Germans. Goldman moved to the Nicola Valley in 1919, purchased 6,550 acres of land, and built up a cattle ranch with over 5,000 head.

(courtesy The BC Adventure Network)

Mount Robson

Location

Mount Robson Provincial Park provides a camping experience that should not be missed. Mount Robson, "the monarch of the Canadian Rockies," is the highest peak in the Rockies at almost 4,000 metres. In 1913 a special Act was passed by the BC legislature to ensure this area of exceptional beauty was preserved for all to encounter and enjoy. The park is easily accessible from the Yellowhead Highway (Highway 5). Services, such as gas, food, and a store, are located in the park itself at Mount Robson Motor Village.

Facilities

There are three campgrounds in the park, and two of them are located at the western end: Robson Meadow has 125 spots; Robson River has 19 spots. Both have flush toilets, showers, and are wheelchair accessible. The third campground is Lucern, 10 kilometres west of the Alberta border, with 32 spots. The sani-station is located at Robson Meadow. Most sites are large, private, and well-situated in the evergreen forest. (Robson River is my favourite, being smaller than Robson Meadow but with all amenities and adjacent to services).

Recreational activities

The spectacular scenery, which consists of lakes, waterfalls, rivers, glaciers, and mountains, makes this a paradise for hikers, climbers, canoeists, and anyone who loves the outdoors. There are over 200 kilometres of hiking trails within the park, one of the most popular being The Valley of the Thousand Waterfalls, which takes explorers past the fantastic azure brightness of Berg Lake and on to views of Tumbling Glacier spectacular waterfalls. I believe this to be one of the best hikes in BC. Boat launches are available at Moose Lake and Yellowhead Lake, but fishing tends to be poor as the glacial waters yield low fish populations. The Mount Robson Visitor Centre at the Mount Robson Viewpoint provides details of all the park's activities and staff to advise on climate and camping conditions.

Additional information

The Indians called Mount Robson "Yuh-hai-has-hun" meaning "Mountain of the Spiral Road." It is unclear whether the park is named after Colin Robertson, a Hudson Bay Company factor and later Member of Parliament, who sent Iroquois fur hunters to the area in 1820, or John Robson, Premier of BC from 1889-1892. This is one of my favourite BC parks, as there is so much to do amongst such breathtaking scenery. In arranging a holiday touring British Columbia, Mount Robson is a lovely destination to head for, but plan to spend at least three nights in order to begin to appreciate its true beauty.

North Thompson River

Location
The most amazing feature of this park is the meeting of two distinctively individual water systems. The 126-hectare provincial park is located where the Thompson and Clearwater Rivers meet, five kilometres south of the town of Clearwater, just off Highway 5. Clearwater has services such as gas, propane, food, and accommodation as well as a number of commercial tour operators.

Facilities
The campground itself is on the banks of the Thompson River among a mixed forest of Douglas-fir, pine, cedar, and spruce. There are 61 camping spots, the more desirable ones being closer to the river. The park is wheelchair accessible, and there is a sani-station.

Recreational activities
A number of short trails lead through the campground all take less than 30 minutes to complete. A wading and swimming area is located on a back eddy where the Clearwater River flows into the North Thompson. BC Parks cautions that during the flood season of June and July currents can be powerful. Canoeing, kayaking, and fishing for rainbow trout and Chinook salmon are also possible here. In addition to the recreational activities available in the park itself, the nearby community of Clearwater offers bikes and canoes to rent, horseback trail rides, and rafting trips.

Additional information
A viewpoint in the park supplies a vista of the distinctive green waters of the Clearwater River meeting those of the muddy, brown Thompson. This was once the site of a Shuswap Indian encampment, and two archaeological sites exist in the park together with signs of native habitation in the form of depressions for pit houses.

Mount Robson.

Paul Lake

Location

Provincial parks near large areas of population often offer the best amenities for family camping, whether it be in a tent or RV. Paul Lake is one such park. Residents of Kamloops and visitors regularly patronize this popular provincial park, conveniently located 24 kilometres northeast of Kamloops. It is found by turning off Highway 5 and following a well-maintained twisting road across a meadow landscape for 17 kilometres. Gas and food are available at the junction of Highway 5; all other needs can be accommodated in Kamloops.

Facilities

The campground has 90 very large, well-maintained, private camping spots set in a lightly forested area of Douglas-fir and aspen, suitable for every type of recreational vehicle, making the park popular with RVs. There is a sani-station, flush and pit toilets, and access for the disabled.

Recreational activities

The lake provides a host of activities, including swimming in a protected area, boating, and fishing. A number of hikes and trails from the campground are possible. The park is particularly appealing to those with young children; it has a playground, horseshoes, and wide grassy areas, and the maze of paved roads connecting the camping facilities ensures fun for the young cyclist.

Additional information

At certain times of the year the park is blessed with a wide array of beautiful wildflowers. (Remember it is forbidden to pick vegetation in the provincial parks.) For good views of the vicinity, campers with stamina are advised to climb Gibraltar Rock. The park's proximity to Kamloops means it is often at capacity, and reservations are not accepted. For some reason, I find this park to have little atmosphere and not as much character as most others. In some respects it appears too ordered and regimented; almost clinical. This is purely a personal interpretation and clearly not one shared by everyone, for when I visited, a number of campers, especially family groups, seemed to be well established. It's just that I find it one of BC's more formal parks.

Shuswap Lake

Location

For people who love water-based activities, Shuswap Lake, with over 1,000 kilometres of waterways, is a real magnet. The provincial park of the same name is one of the larger BC Parks and accommodates 271 vehicles, (in 1995 registering over 24,000 camping parties). It is conveniently located 90 kilometres east of Kamloops on Highway 1 at Squailax. A 20-kilometre paved road leads to the campground. Some supplies can be found at a store adjacent to the entrance of the park, while more comprehensive supplies are found in Sorrento, 35 kilometres away.

Facilities

Because Shuswap Lake is one of BC's largest provincial parks, the facilities offered here are comprehensive and include 271 camping spots suitable for every type of recreational vehicle, flush and pit toilets, sani-station, showers, and full access for the disabled. Reservations are accepted, and BC Parks describes Shuswap Lake as operating at capacity from mid-July to Labour Day.

Recreational activities

One of the most popular recreational pursuits here is cycling as there are over 11 kilometres of paved road in the park itself. Water sports are also actively undertaken on the one kilometre of beach and designated swimming area. There is a boat launch, and two kilometres offshore is Copper Island, which contains a hiking trail and lookout. Anglers can fish in the lake and share it with windsurfers and paddlers. To entertain the entire family there is an adventure play area, a visitor centre, and interpretive programs. Commercial recreational activities (for example kayak rentals and go-carts) are also easily accessible in the North Shuswap and surrounding area.

Additional information

While there is no overnight boat mooring at Shuswap Lake, the nearby Shuswap Lake Provincial Marine Park offers this facility, as well as six separate developed and eight undeveloped camping locations along all four arms of the lake. As mentioned above, this area is extremely popular during the summer months and may not be to everyone's taste at that time as it presents the more commercial side of camping in BC Parks. For those who want to experience the delights of the lake from a quieter vantage point, Herald and Silver Beach Provincial Parks provide tranquil alternatives.

(courtesy BC Parks)

Silver Beach

Location

Campers who wish to enjoy the waters but not the crowds of Shuswap Lake should head for Silver Beach. This somewhat remote provincial park is located 65 kilometres from Scotch Creek. Turn off Highway 1 just east of Squailax and take the paved road to Scotch Creek. The road to the park from Scotch Creek is only partially paved. Gas and limited provisions are available near the campground.

Facilities

There are 30 vehicle/tent campsites and five walk-in campsites located amongst a forest of Douglas-fir and aspen at the head of the Seymour Arm of the Shuswap Lake. Silver Beach contains the basic facilities found in BC Parks (pit toilets, picnic tables, water, wood, fire pit).

Recreational activities

As this quiet campground is at the northern end of Shuswap Lake all activities related to the lake can be enjoyed here: swimming, fishing (for trout amongst others), boating, canoeing, windsurfing, water-skiing, etc. In August and September it is possible to view sockeye salmon spawning in the Seymour River, which runs into the lake near the campground. Wildfowl observation is also good.

Additional information

The remains of an old gold rush town of the late nineteenth century can be seen here if you are prepared to navigate a somewhat overgrown trail. With its beautiful sandy beaches this campground is popular with sailors and houseboaters who are exploring the lake, so expect to share your tranquillity with more than just your fellow dry-land campers. Houseboating is a very popular activity on the four arms of the Shuswap. At the height of the season as many as 350 are navigating the waters of the lake. Silver Beach provides a quieter and less commercialized view of Shuswap Lake than Shuswap Lake Provincial Park but does not have all the facilities that the larger park offers.

(courtesy BC Parks)

Skihist

Location
Anyone stopping here will be rewarded with brilliant views of the Thompson Canyon, but be sure to remember the sun screen as Skihist is situated in an area prone to very high summer temperatures. This quaint 33-hectare provincial park is found eight kilometres east of Lytton, which houses services, on Highway 1.

Facilities
Fifty-six well-positioned camping spots set in a lightly forested area high above the Thompson and Fraser Rivers are available. The park has both pit and flush toilets; it has a sani-station and is wheelchair accessible. There is a large day-use area, which is a popular resting place in the summer.

Recreational activities
Recreational activities in the park are limited to discovering Saskatoon berries, which are plentiful at certain times, taking photographs, admiring the fantastic views, and looking for the elk which have been introduced to the area. The campground is a good base for those who wish to try the whitewater rafting easily arranged through commercial businesses in Lytton and Spences Bridge.

Additional information
Skihist Provincial Park includes part of the old Cariboo Wagon Road used by the early pioneers of the province. Its main attraction must be the fantastic views of the Thompson Canyon, where water gushing over thousands of years has cut into the pre-glacial valley floor. (The fact it has flush toilets is another attraction). Lytton, at the junction of the Fraser and Thompson Rivers, claims to be the official hot spot in Canada, although the claim is disputed by Lillooet to the north. As neither has a weather station, the debate continues. Be prepared for some hot days if visiting Skihist in the peak summer months.

(courtesy The BC Adventure Network)

Steelhead

Location
Set in an almost desert environment, Steelhead, which saw its first year of operation in 1997, really is the baby of provincial parks. It provides an excellent base location to explore the town of Kamloops, Kamloops Lake, the mighty Thompson River, and the surrounding plateau scenery. The campground is found 45 kilometres west of Kamloops on Highway 1, just west of Savona, which has food, gas, and supplies.

Facilities
The campground is situated at the outflow of Kamloops Lake. Thirty-two camping spots are available, in addition to flush toilets and showers. The park is wheelchair accessible. Reservations are not accepted.

Recreational activities
Residents of these camping spots can enjoy swimming and canoeing in Kamloops Lake in addition to fishing at this location and in the many plateau lakes in the region. There is no boat launch. Naturalists appreciate the wildlife in the area, which includes deer, elk, and mountain sheep in addition to migratory waterfowl, shorebirds, and songbirds. The town of Kamloops is only a short drive away and is the major centre of the region. Just south of the campground is the community of Logan Lake, where fascinating tours of the Highland Valley Copper Mine can be taken.

Additional information
BC Parks should be sincerely thanked for establishing a number of additional campgrounds in the High Country Region in 1997. Steelhead is the most developed; other recent additions are Momich, Tunkwa, and Roche Lake. All were previously forestry campsites, but in 1997 BC Parks became responsible for their administration. These other locations only have primitive camping facilities (see Additional Campgrounds below). If staying in this region, be prepared for some very high temperatures and remember to pack the sun screen.

Spahats Creek

Location

"Spahats" is the local Indian name for "bear," so watch out for these beasts at this 306-hectare provincial park. Spahats is located approximately 11 kilometres north of Clearwater, off Highway 5 on a paved road access (en route to Wells Gray Provincial Park). Services can be found in Clearwater.

Facilities

The facilities provided here are limited to the basic ones found in BC Parks (pit toilets, wood, water, picnic tables, fire pit). Twenty well-spaced, private camping spots are available within a forested area.

Recreational activities

Spahats Creek's main attraction is the magnificent Spahats Creek Falls. From a lookout, visitors can view the 122-metre-deep canyon carved by Spahats Creek to the 61-metre falls as they cascade down the volcanic precipice to the Clearwater River below. Be sure to remember a camera to record this spectacle. An interpretive display describes the geology of the area. A number of hiking trails lead from this location, and access to Wells Gray Provincial Park is only a short drive away. Fishing in the creek is also possible.

Additional information

This area of the North Thompson is becoming increasingly popular for outdoors people who come to experience the acres upon acres of undisturbed forest, an abundance of lakes, rivers, and streams, fantastic mountain scenery, miles upon miles of trails, and moderate summertime temperatures. As this park is so close to one of BC's largest parks, Wells Gray, known as "the waterfall park," the facilities, recreational pursuits, and breathtaking scenery offered by this near neighbour are easily accessible. Campers can therefore savour the best of two beautiful provincial parks.

Stake-McConnell Lakes

Location
For those who enjoy fly fishing, or for those who want to attempt this sport, Stake-McConnell is the place to be. This site used to be under the auspices of BC Forests, but over the last ten years has been administered by BC Parks. It can be found 18 kilometres southwest of Kamloops by turning off Highway 5 at the Lac Le Jeune exit. The nearest services are in Kamloops.

Facilities
The small campground has just ten spots and the basic facilities found in BC Parks (firewood, pit toilets, water, picnic table, cooking pit).

Recreational activities
The park includes several small lakes, including McConnell and Stake Lakes which give the park its name and from which it is possible to fish, swim, mountain bike, and canoe/kayak. Hiking trails also lead from the area. It is difficult to believe that the busy city of Kamloops is less than 20 kilometres from this tranquillity. Dating back to 1812, Kamloops was established as a fur-trading post; today much of the town's early development has been buried under housing development. The Kamloops Museum is located in a mid-nineteenth century fur-trade cabin, the oldest building in town, and contains displays of native history, fur traders' experiences, pioneer living, and transportation.

Additional information
This park is located only a few kilometres north of Lac Le Jeune, which is larger and more developed. For those seeking a quiet fishing retreat, Stake-McConnell Lakes Park is ideal, and as already mentioned, it is reputed to have excellent fly fishing. For those with young children or a larger recreational vehicle, Lac Le Jeune would be the preferred location.

Lake Mahood, Wells Gray Provincial Park. (courtesy BC Parks)

Wells Gray

Location

There are hundreds of things to see and do at Wells Gray. BC Parks literature describes it as a "vast, untamed and primitive wilderness exceeding 520,000 hectares in area and encompassing the greater part of the Clearwater River Watershed." The park contains two large river systems, five huge lakes, numerous small lakes, streams, waterways, rapids, and waterfalls. The main entrance to Wells Gray is 40 kilometres from the community of Clearwater on a paved access road. The road from Helmken Falls to Clearwater Lake is gravel. The park can also be reached by travelling 88 kilometres on a secondary road from 100 Mile House. One further entrance from Blue River is also possible. Services are located at Clearwater and 100 Mile House.

Facilities

In addition to numerous wilderness camping spots, there are four campgrounds in the park. Three campgrounds are accessed from the Clearwater approach road and include Dawson Falls, which has 10 units, Clearwater Lake, which has 32 spots, and Falls Creek with 41 units. A sani-station is available at Clearwater Lake. The fourth campground is reached from the 100 Mile House entrance (off Highway 97) and has 32 spots. Facilities consist of the basic ones found in BC Parks (pit toilets, wood, water, picnic tables, fire pit).

Recreational activities

As Wells Gray is BC's fourth largest provincial park there exists a wealth of things to see and do. Numerous trails run through the park and lead to waterfalls and creeks; some of the trails are open to mountain bikes. Boat launches are provided at Mahood and Clearwater Lake, and canoeing and kayaking is very popular in the park (powerboats are prohibited on Murtle Lake). Fishing is reputed to be good in Canim River, Mahood Lake, Murtle Lake, and the Murtle River.

Additional information

The park, named after the Honourable A. Wells Gray, Minister of Lands for BC from 1933 to 1941, displays a landscape formed by volcanoes and water. It is impossible to count the number of waterfalls in the park, but two of the best known are Helmcken Falls and Dawson Falls, which are spectacular in both winter and summer. BC Parks publishes a number of informative leaflets on the recreational activities available here, and this information is a must for anyone wanting to gain maximum benefit from a holiday. A Travel Information Centre at the junction of Highway 5 and Clearwater Valley Road supplies these details.

Yard Creek

Location

At certain times of the year, campers can feast their eyes (but not their lips) on a fantastic array of mushrooms that flourish in the vicinity of Yard Creek. This is one of a number of provincial park campgrounds adjacent to Highway 1 that are primarily used for overnight stops. Yard Creek is conveniently situated 60 kilometres west of Revelstoke and ten kilometres east of Sicamous on Highway 1. The nearest services are at Sicamuos.

Facilities

The 65 private camping spots available in this 61-hectare park can accommodate every type of recreational vehicle. The campsites are set in pleasantly forested parkland of hemlock and cedar. There is a sani-station and flush and pit toilets. The park is not wheelchair accessible.

Recreational activities

Fishing at this location is possible but not great as the waters of Yard Creek are very cold. A hiking trail along the creek itself is a pleasant relief from a day's long drive. As previously stated, the area is known for its mushrooms, which can grow in abundance in certain locations, (but remember, collecting plants in BC Parks is prohibited). The town of Sicamous, which takes its name from the Salish language and means "narrow" or "squeezed," is ten kilometres away. Sicamous has a sternwheeler on which tours of Shuswap Lake can be enjoyed.

Additional information

Sicamous used to be known as a railway construction depot but is now the houseboat capital of Canada, with almost 350 houseboats available to rent for vacationers to explore the waters of Shuswap Lake and the surrounding mountain scenery. The road from Sicamous to Revelstoke marks a dramatic change in scenery as the peaks of the Rocky Mountains come into view and dominate the horizon. Yard Creek is a convenient, well-situated stopover for those travelling on Highway 1.

Additional Campgrounds

Cinnemousun Narrows Marine

Accessible only by boat, this campground is found where the four arms of Shuswap Lake meet. Twenty-eight walk-in spots exist at this most popular region of the lake. Pit toilets, a marine sani-station, and fresh water are supplied, but there is no firewood. There is a lovely sandy beach and a hiking trail leads to a vantage area with good views of the lake.

Momich

Thirty camping spots are available at this remote location, which does not have water or firewood but does have four pit toilets. There is a boat launch, swimming, fishing, and canoeing. The area features a lovely, white sandy beach and the chance to see eagles. Situated at the northern end of beautiful Adams Lake, Momich can be reached either from the Trans-Canada Highway at Squilax, then 95 kilometres of forestry road, or from Barriere on Highway 5 and 80 kilometres of forestry road.

Niskonlith Lake

Characterized by a Douglas-fir and cottonwood tree environment, Niskonlith Lake is found eight kilometres southeast of Chase off Highway 1 on a somewhat rough gravel road. There is no tap or pump water at the site, which accommodates 32 spots; there are, however, six pit toilets, picnic tables, fire pits, and wood. Fishing for rainbow trout, hiking, and bird-watching (ospreys nest in the area) are popular activities here.

Roche Lake

Roche Lake Provincial Park protects a series of world-class trout fishing lakes. It is situated 36 kilometres (7 kilometres on gravel road) southeast of Kamloops off Highway 5A at the north end of Trapp Lake. Seventy-five camping spots are provided in two campgrounds. No drinking water or firewood is supplied. The park has swimming, fishing, canoeing, and boating opportunities and is equipped with a boat launch.

Shuswap Lake Marine

This campground has no vehicle access but boasts 44 walk-in campsites at three locations: Two Mile Creek (8); Anstrey Arm (20); and Salmon Arm (16). Access is only available from the waters of Shuswap Lake. Pit toilets are provided, but there is no fresh water or firewood. Fishing, swimming, and hiking are the primary recreational activities.

Tunkwa Lake

Camping, fishing, hiking, nature study, wildlife viewing, horseback riding, and even—if the time is right—snowmobiling can all be enjoyed here. The campground has 80 spots and is found midway between Savona and Logan Lake, accessed by a short gravel road. Pit toilets are provided, but there is no water, firewood, or sani-station. Tunkwa and Leighton Lakes are known primarily for their excellent trout fishing. The site was formerly a forestry campground and was taken over by BC Parks in 1996.

7 Cariboo Country

Steeped in the history of the Gold Rush and covering an area of over 100,000 square kilometres, the Cariboo region includes campgrounds situated on Highway 97 north of Cache Creek to Prince George. This section of road is known as the Gold Rush Trail after the pioneers who travelled it in search of precious metal. Today, many buildings and historical markers recount the days of this original wagon road first built in 1860. The Cariboo region also includes campgrounds found on minor roads off this major route and incorporates an area characterized by rolling hills, grasslands, over 8,000 lakes, and numerous rivers stretching from the foothills of the Rockies to the Pacific coast. Recently the area has become known for its many guest ranches and for being "cowboy country," so go—and ride 'em cowboy!

Grubstake Store at Barkerville.

Barkerville

Location

For those wanting to visit the historic gold rush town of Barkerville this provincial park provides an excellent base. Barkerville was once the largest town west of Chicago and north of San Francisco. The park is situated 89 kilometres east of Quesnel on a paved and scenic road (Highway 26) and within a few kilometres of Wells, where a comprehensive range of services can be found.

Facilities

There are 170 campsites at three locations within this provincial park. The two campgrounds nearest to the historic town are Lowhee, with 87 quite open and sparsely treed sites, and Government Hill, with 25 very open, small, functional sites offering little privacy. A sani-station, showers, and flush toilets are available at Lowhee. The small "Grubstake" Store is located adjacent to these two sites. I prefer the third campground, Forest Rose, with 56 sites which are larger and more private. There are a number of pull-through spots, and this location also has showers and flush toilets. The campground is wheelchair accessible and reservations are accepted.

Recreational activities

Although there are a few walking and hiking trails in the area and fish can be caught in the nearby rivers and lakes, the main draw is the reconstructed and faithfully restored 1870s gold rush town. Barkerville houses over 40 pre-1900 buildings and provides an active interpretive program which successfully conveys the life of a gold rush pioneer. Actors dressed in the clothing of the period wander the historical streets and interact with visitors, providing thousands of people every year with an enjoyable experience of a bygone era.

Additional information

BC Parks manages the three campgrounds in the area but not the Barkerville historical town. Although this provincial park is not the most beautiful BC has to offer, it provides easy access to an important element of the province's history. While staying here it is possible to try your luck at panning for gold. The Grubstake Store between Lowhee and Government Hill campgrounds sells pans, but they are more reasonably priced in Wells. The journey from Highway 97 is scenic and there are a number of historical markers with information about the region's rich past. The nearby town of Wells has a number of buildings that date back to the early part of the century, and many are being slowly restored, making Wells an interesting community to explore.

A brand new Heritage House book, *Goldpanning Creeks of the Cariboo* tells the secrets of a retired prospector and his discovery sites along six of the most productive creeks in the Cariboo.

Big Bar Lake

Location

The people who walked the land around Big Bar Lake before the time of the late twentieth century camper were native hunters, cowboys, cattle rustlers, and gold prospectors. According to local legends, their ghosts can often be seen and heard, so be attentive when you stay here. Big Bar Lake is on the southern edge of the Fraser Plateau, a landscape formed millions of years ago by debris left by glaciers. Evidence of the ice age can be seen at the west of the lake, where gravel eskers remain; much of the topography owes its development to this geological period. To reach Big Bar Lake it is necessary to drive eight kilometres north of Clinton on Highway 97 and then take a gravel road west for 34 kilometres to the park itself. The nearest services can be found at 70 Mile House.

Facilities

The park has two campgrounds with a total of 33 spots. Fifteen sites are on the lakeshore, with the remaining ones located in the forest above the lake. There is no sani-station and facilities are basic (fire pit, picnic tables, wood, water, pit toilets).

Recreational activities

A naturalist's delight, the area is characterized by forests of lodgepole pine and spruce. This vegetation provides an excellent habitat for wildlife, including mule deer, black bear, cougar, lynx, marmots, and snowshoe hares. Easy access to the lake means boating, swimming, and fishing are possible and the lake is stocked annually with rainbow trout. A two-kilometre trail provides excellent waterfowl and bird-watching, facilitated by a water control structure that was built by Ducks Unlimited to encourage nesting. Longer hikes are also possible.

Additional information

Big Bar Lake Park covers 332 hectares. The area was originally settled by the nomadic Salish Indians; nowadays it is known as typical rolling hill ranching country, and trail rides can be arranged through the numerous guest ranches located in the area. These ranches operate year-round and also offer gold-panning excursions, skiing, riding lessons, and pack trips. The inclusion of snowshoe hares in the list of wildlife found around Big Bar Lake should forewarn you: early in the season beautiful warm days can develop into clear, cold nights. So act like a cowboy and remember the longjohns if you'll be camping under canvas.

Bowron Lake

Location
This world-renowned park's famous Bowron Lake canoe circuit covers over 116 kilometres around 11 different lakes, an excursion which takes between between seven and ten days. The campground is located 113 kilometres east of Quesnel, 18 kilometres past the end of Highway 16 on a gravel road. Two commercial resorts on Bowron Lake offer a selection of services including food and camping supplies, while a full range can be found in Wells, 23 kilometres away.

Facilities
Twenty-five campsites suitable for vehicles and tents are located near the park entrance. Facilities are basic (firewood, picnic tables, fire pit, water, and pit toilets), but reservations are accepted. Anyone planning to canoe the circuit can reserve by phoning 250-992-3111. There are 103 wilderness/walk-in sites in this park of 123,117 hectares.

Recreational activities
Near the campground it is possible to swim, fish for Dolly Varden, rainbow trout, and lake char, and of course to canoe. Boat rentals are available nearby. Wildlife includes moose, deer, caribou, black and grizzly bears, and coyotes. There are bald and golden eagles, ospreys and hawks, as well as a wealth of waterfowl and songbirds.

Additional information
To be able to fully appreciate the beauty of Bowron Lake Provincial Park, you should spend a week or more here. The park's reputation grows annually, both within North America and Europe; consequently it becomes increasingly difficult to ensure a reservation. Advance planning is required if you plan to canoe the circuit. For more detail, see Richard Wrights *Bowron Lake Provincial Park* (Heritage House). For those who just want to visit the area, it may be easier to stay at Barkerville. Wells is a neat little community from which canoe rental companies also operate, delivering the canoes and kayaks to Bowron Lake for those interested in paddling the circuit, or even for those who just want to spend a day enjoying the beauty of the area.

(courtesy BC Parks)

Bridge Lake

Location

The area is known as the "Interlakes District" and is an angler's paradise. The hundreds of lakes that cover the landscape offer fishing potential primarily for eastern brook and lake trout, burbot, and kokanee. Bridge Lake Provincial Park was established by BC Parks in 1957 and covers a modest six hectares. There are two main ways to reach Bridge Lake. The first entails turning off Highway 97 east of 93 Mile House on Highway 24. The campground is 50 kilometres east of Highway 97. The second way is to turn off Highway 5 at Little Fort and to travel west on Highway 24. Full services are available at 100 Mile House.

Facilities

Twenty vehicle/tent sites and seven walk-in campsites are available. The sites are large, set amongst trees, and have views of the lake. Facilities are basic and consist of firewood, picnic tables, fire pit, water, and pit toilets. There is no sani-station.

Recreational activities

Activities at this location include fishing for burbot, lake and rainbow trout (there is a boat launch) and swimming. The lake is also ideal for canoeing and kayaking. A small hiking trail skirts the lakeside, and there is an archaeological site in the park itself.

Additional information

Recently a number of resorts have developed in the area and these now offer holiday excursions. The easily accessible location from two main highways means that this campground is a quiet stop-off for the traveller during the busy peak months of July and August. The location seems to be particularly popular with anglers, who perhaps hope to catch a fish or two while having a relaxing break away from the steering wheel.

Ben 1, Dad 0; Dinner for six! (courtesy Dennis Herd)

Bull Canyon

Location

The campground at Bull Canyon Provincial Park is in a particularly beautiful setting on the Fraser Plateau by the Chilcotin River and provides an excellent overnight stop for those travelling between Williams Lake and Bella Coola. This pleasantly treed 123-hectare park is found ten kilometres west of Alexis Creek on Highway 20. The nearest full range of services are at Williams Lake 122 kilometres away, but gas and basic food items can be purchased at Alexis Creek.

Facilities

Twenty basic campsites are located in an open camping area overlooking the Chilcotin River. Facilities are only the most rudimentary found in BC parks (wood, water, fire pit, picnic tables, pit toilets). There is no sani-station and water is obtained from a pump.

Recreational activities

Fishing is possible from the river as is canoeing and kayaking. Lakes in the area also provide access to these recreational pursuits. The area is good for bird-watching and wildlife viewing, and a wonderful array of wildflowers can be found here at certain times of the year, however in winter, this region can experience some very cold temperatures, sometimes as low as -50 degrees centigrade.

Additional information

While staying at another provincial park I met a very excited retired gentleman from Germany who had been holidaying by RV in BC for the last ten years and claimed to have travelled on every road other than Highway 20, but this year he was going to undertake that journey. One of the more pleasant aspects of staying in BC Provincial Parks is the people you meet from all areas of the world and the advice they give you on travelling in the province and which campgrounds are their favourites.

Canim Beach

Location

Moose are reputed to be quite common here. Unfortunately, I seem to have trouble spotting any type of animal wherever they are said to be easily spotted, and therefore I have yet to see any moose at Canim Beach. Others may have more luck. The lack of moose sightings on my visit was easily compensated for by the excellent views of the Quesnel Highlands leading on to the Cariboo Mountains. Canim Beach can be found by travelling 43 kilometres east of 100 Mile House on paved road access. A full range of services are available at 100 Mile House with more limited needs being furnished by the few local communities.

Facilities

A total of 16 sites are available at Canim Beach; seven are for vehicles/ tents, while nine are walk-in spots at the beach. All have views of the lake. There is no sani-station and facilities consist of the basic ones found in provincial parks (firewood, picnic tables, fire pit, water, and pit toilets).

Recreational activities

Leisure pursuits centre around the 37-kilometre-long lake and include swimming, fishing, and boating. The beach is a mixture of gravel and pebbles, and the water level of the lake can fluctuate considerably during the camping seasons. Although there is no boat launch at the park itself, one is available at the end of nearby Harrinam Road. Water-skiing is possible at this location. Many of the nearby private resorts offer boat, kayak, and canoe rentals.

Additional information

"Canim" means "canoe" in the Shuswap language. The views from this campground are very good, and as the lake is one of the larger in the region it is a magnet for water sports. Generally, though, in being away from the major route, Canim Beach Provincial Park offers a very gentle and relaxing stay.

(courtesy The BC Adventure Network)

Downing

Location
The scenery from this campground is quite lovely. Mount Bowman, which can be seen to the north, is at 2243 metres the highest mountain in the Marble Range. Downing Park almost completely encircles Kelly Lake and can be found 18 kilometres southwest of Clinton off Highway 97 on a paved road. Services are available at the quaint town of Clinton and include restaurants, post office, grocery store, pub, bakery, and gas.

Facilities
There are 25 campsites on an open grassy area with views of the lake. An additional 22 wilderness sites also exist in the park. There is no sani-station, wheelchair accessibility is limited, and facilities are restricted to the basic ones found in BC Parks (fire pit, picnic tables, wood, water, pit toilets).

Recreational activities
Recreational activities include fishing for rainbow trout, hiking, a small beach, sunbathing, and swimming. There is no public boat launch. The nearby community of Clinton has a small museum and excellent ice cream bar and is a pleasant place to while away a few hours. It also boasts the largest log-constructed building in BC.

Additional information
Downing Park, which covers approximately 100 hectares, was donated by C. S. Downing in 1970, and his family still owns the adjoining property. BC Rail runs along one side of the lake so you may be lulled to sleep by the sound of trains. For those who do not have time to stay, this site makes an ideal spot to rest, picnic, and bathe and is particularly inviting to travellers who have taken the unpaved road between Pavilion, north of Lillooet, to Clinton. Drivers should be warned that the unpaved road between Downing Park and Pavilion is at times very steep and has hairpin bends which can be nerve-wracking. Pavilion has a beautiful little church well worth a photograph.

The picnic tables are not always no uninviting in this picnic shelter. (courtesy The BC Adventure Network).

Green Lake

Location

The Green Lake area was recognized as bountiful by Canada's indigenous population many years ago; today campers of every age continue to appreciate its bounty. Green Lake Provincial Park is situated among groves of aspen and lodgepole pine 15 kilometres northeast of 70 Mile House on a paved road, adjacent to the 14-kilometre lake from which it takes its name. Three campgrounds are available on both sides of the lake. Information about the exact location of the campgrounds is available at the road junction ten kilometres east of 70 Mile House. Services are available at 70 Mile House.

Facilities

Each of Green Lake's three campgrounds has something different to offer. The most popular, Arrowhead, is relatively small and offers 16 spots, all situated on the beach front. (Probably the best family swimming is to be found here.) The second camping area is Emerald Bay. Like Arrowhead, Emerald Bay is situated on North Green Lake Road but is larger, with 51 sites, a number of them on the water's edge. Sunset View campground has 54 sites and is on South Green Lake Road. All spots are relatively private and situated amongst aspen trees. There is limited access for the disabled and a sani-station. Some sites at Emerald Bay can be reserved.

Recreational activities

Boredom should not be a problem here as there are numerous activities to entertain every age group. The lake has moderately good fishing for rainbow trout and is restocked annually. There is a boat launch at Emerald Bay and water-skiing is allowed, but please keep well away from swimming areas. Children's playgrounds exist at both Emerald Bay and Sunset View and there are trails leading from the park for hikes. The shallow west area of the lake attracts numerous waterfowl and migratory birds and is a magnet for ornithologists.

Additional information

Green Lake is 14 kilometres long and averages 1.5 kilometres in width. It has minimum outflow enabling a high buildup of algae and other microorganisms which, along with the composition of the water itself, give the lake it's greenish tinge. Information from BC Parks suggests using the park in the spring, when large rainbow trout spawning in the creeks attract large numbers of bald eagles, and in the fall, when the aspens turn fantastic shades of red and orange, each occurrence being quite beautiful for those with an appreciative eye (or a camera at hand).

Green Lake (right) offers a variety
of activities to enjoy.
(courtesy The BC Adventure Network)

Horsefly Lake

Location

Horsefly Lake is a delightful 148-hectare park set amongst an assortment of trees including western hemlock, redcedars, various spruce and subalpine fir. Access is achieved by turning off Highway 97 at 150 Mile House and travelling 52 kilometres on paved road to Horsefly, then 13 kilometres along a good gravel road to the park. Services at Horsefly include a cafe, grocery store, and gas station.

Facilities

The campground has 23 private sites in a coniferous forest. There is no sani-station and only the basic facilities found in BC Parks exist (pit toilets, wood, water, picnic tables, fire pit).

Recreational activities

This location offers a number of pastimes to pursue. Trails lead to Viewland Mountain and Eureka Park; details on these are available at the information board at the park entrance. Anglers visit the park to fish for rainbow trout in Horsefly Lake and in the smaller adjacent lakes. Canoeing and boating are possible and there is a boat launch. The beach has a change room for swimmers. Just outside the community of Horsefly there are spawning channels with a system of dikes for walking and viewing. The best viewing opportunity is mid-September when the sockeye are spawning.

Additional information

This area was once a centre for gold mining. (Jim Lewis and Charles Hart have written a fascinating book, *Gold Panning in the Cariboo*, which details the exploits of the early prospectors.) Horsefly was originally called Harpers Camp after one of the early settlers but was renamed by later pioneers who discovered one of its drawbacks. In 1859 the first gold in the Cariboo was discovered here, and today some people continue to be drawn to the area in search of gold. The park covers a considerable area, most of which is semi-wilderness and inaccessible to the visitor.

Lac la Hache

Location

Lac la Hache, also known as "Kumatakwa," means "axe lake," and numerous stories have been advanced to explain how this name came to be. According to one, the name is simply based on the shape of the lake; another story holds that it gained its name by a trapper losing his axe through the frozen lake when trying to reach water. The park is situated 12 kilometres north of the community of Lac la Hache on Highway 97 where services can be found. There is a small store opposite the campground.

Facilities

The facilities here are good and include 83 campsites, flush toilets, tap water, and a sani-station. All sites are large, relatively private, and set in open Douglas-fir and aspen woodlands. Some sites are close to the road, however, and it is possible there to hear the traffic from the busy Highway 97.

Recreational activities

A number of activities are provided at this campground. Small trails lead around the vicinity, and from these it is possible to see and walk remnants of the historic Cariboo Wagon Road. There is an adventure playground, and interpretive programs are offered during the summer. The lake is popular for water-skiing, boating, and fishing. Rainbow trout, kokanee, and burbot can be caught. There is a beach and swimming area. (Be aware that the campground is across the road from the lake and that vehicles can and do travel at speed along this stretch of highway.) Three kilometres north of the campground is the Cariboo Nature Park, which is an excellent location for bird-watching. Lac la Hache also claims to be BC's longest town. Unfortunately, with the exception of some small cafes and restaurants, I find there is little to attract the visitor.

Additional information

I am romantically attached to this park as it was the first BC provincial park I stayed in. On that initial occasion, and on the rare occasions I have had the opportunity to visit again, I have been impressed with the friendly and informative camp hosts. The lack of provincial parks on Highway 97, coupled with good family facilities, makes this a popular location. The small store is a magnet for children walking to and from the lake, and during the early evening pop and candy would appear to be the store's most popular lines. In 1997 reservations at this provincial park were not accepted.

Loon Lake

Location

While camping for many means cooking over an open fire, sometimes the craving for non-barbecued cuisine takes over and alternatives are sought. At Loon Lake the number of private lodges and facilities in the area enables campers to exercise this option if they so desire. Set among ponderosa pine and Douglas-fir, this three-hectare provincial park is approximately 50 kilometres northeast of Cache Creek on a paved road access, 20 kilometres east of 20 Mile House. The small

The Chef—Andrew Dewberry.

community of Loon Lake provides a number of services, including restaurants, a small store, and fishing supplies. Gas and propane, though, must be purchased at Cache Creek or Clinton.

Facilities

There are only 14 campsites here, quite closely spaced and open. Six are pull-through sites. The campground is situated on the warm south-facing side of the lake with the campsites overlooking the waters. Seven sites have tent pads. There is no sani-station, and facilities are limited to the basic ones found in provincial parks, (fire pit, picnic tables, wood, water, pit toilets).

Recreational activities

The 12-kilometre-long, 40-metre-wide lake is the main recreational venue here and offers swimming, fishing, and boating. There is an undeveloped boat launch off Steven's Road; alternatively the private campgrounds provide access to their boat launches for a fee. From June to September the fishing for rainbow trout is excellent. An archeological site exists within the park's boundaries.

Additional information

The adjacent communities also supply boat rentals for those who do not have their own craft. The Loon Creek Hatchery rears Chinook and steelhead and is worth a visit; it is located prior to the campground. Tenters should be aware that the warm fall or spring days can turn into bitterly cold nights in this region, so make sure you get well wrapped up if visiting in these seasons. Loon Lake is an excellent spot to fish and relax.

Marble Canyon

Location

Marble Canyon Provincial Park is popular with rock climbers who are attracted to the area for its rugged terrain. It is not difficult to see why mountaineers and others chose to visit this park nestled on a lakeside below towering limestone cliffs and amongst the beautiful scenery of Marble Canyon. The campground is found by travelling 40 kilometres west of Cache Creek along Highway 12. It is about 35 kilometres northeast of Lillooet. Services are available at Cache Creek or Lillooet.

Facilities

There are 26 relatively small gravel campsites with no privacy, some directly overlooking the lake. The services provided are limited to the basic ones found in BC parks (pit toilets, picnic tables, wood, water, fire pit).

Recreational activities

Leisure activities include fishing, swimming, kayaking, and canoeing. Only electric motors are permitted on the lake. Along the side of the lake there is a trail which leads to a waterfall. Two archaeological sites where Indian pictographs have been found are located in the park. In addition, those interested in fauna and flora should find the vegetation and the bird and animal life fascinating.

Additional information

Reaching this campground is a beautiful and scenic drive. Close to Lillooet, travellers see some of the ginseng farms for which BC has now become known. These are characterized by the vast expanse of black plastic. At the junction of Highway 97 and Highway 99, the historical 1861 Hat Creek Ranch, an original stopping place on the Cariboo Wagon Road, offers guided tours. The area is noted for it's rock formations, scenery, and the beautiful lake. The disadvantage in camping here is the close proximity of the campsite to the road; although the route is not tremendously busy, campers may be kept awake by the sound of traffic. When I stayed here noise was not a problem, and we enjoyed an evening meal cooked at the lakeside as our campsite was on the water's edge. BC Parks warns that wasps can be a problem here, although these annoying insects never seem to dampen visitors' enthusiasm for the location. As always, black bears inhabit the vicinity.

(courtesy BC Parks)

140

Ten Mile Lake

Location
Looking for somewhere to camp with the children? Then look no further than Ten Mile Lake. Situated in an area of pine and aspen forest 11 kilometres north of Quesnel on Highway 97, this large campground is popular with both RVers and tenters, and it is particularly appealing for those with little ones to entertain. All needs can be met in Quesnel.

Facilities
Excellent facilities exist at this location and include a sani-station, flush toilets, a pressure water system, showers, and access for the disabled. There are two campgrounds offering 131 spaces. One is near the lakeshore and the other (which has slightly larger spots) is set among pine trees. There are a number of pull-through sites and reservations are accepted.

Recreational activities
As is common among the larger provincial parks, a variety of leisure pursuits for both old and young are available, but, as mentioned above, Ten Mile Lake is particularly attractive for those with children. A gently sloping sandy beach provides easy access for swimming; there is a boat launch and fishing possibilities. An extensive network of trails leads explorers through mixed forest to the site of a beaver dam and lodge. Ducks Unlimited have been placing nesting boxes in this area to encourage wildlife. There is a children's play area and horseshoes.

Additional information
At the turn of the century Ten Mile Lake was a milepost for the Pacific Great Eastern Railway, evidence of which can still be seen in the day-use area. This campground is a delight, as there are numerous activities within the park itself as well as in the immediate vicinity. The town of Quesnel, named after Jules Maurice Quesnelle, a member of Simon Fraser's exploration party, is only a short distance away. It is rich in pioneer gold-rush history and has a museum, historical markers, and, for those less interested in the past, a couple of golf courses. Ten Mile Lake is heavily used in winter for cross-country skiing and other outdoor activities.

(courtesy The BC Adventure Network)

Tweedsmuir (South)

Location

It is not just people who are attracted to this area. In salmon spawning season, grizzly bears can often be seen fishing in the numerous streams which flow through Tweedsmuir, so be careful. Tweedsmuir, the largest park in the province, is named after the 15th Governor General of Canada, John Buchan, Baron Tweedsmuir of Elsfield, who travelled in the area in 1937 and was impressed by its beauty. The park is divided into north and south regions with only the south being accessible by road. This southern section is located on Highway 20 on the Williams Lake to Bella Coola road, 51 kilometres from Bella Coola, where services are found. Supplies such as gas, food, accommodation, restaurants, and canoe rentals can be obtained close to the park itself.

Facilities

There are two campgrounds accessible from Highway 20. Atnarko River has 28 sites set amidst a grove of old-growth Douglas-fir, 28 kilometres from the eastern entrance of the park. Fisheries Pool campground, located near to Stuie, 44 kilometres from the park's eastern entrance, has 14. Facilities include a sani-station, firewood, picnic tables, fire pit, pump water, and pit toilets.

Recreational activities

As one would expect in a provincial park of this size, there is a wealth of things to see and do. The park is home to a wide variety of wildlife including deer, moose, caribou, black and grizzly bears, wolf, and cougar. Rainbow trout, cutthroat trout, and Dolly Varden are found in the park's many lakes and streams, while the Atnarko and Dean Rivers are spawning grounds for trout and salmon. Water sports, including swimming, canoeing, and kayaking, are possible, and there is a boat launch at Fisheries Pool. The area is known as one of the most outstanding for alpine hiking in BC, and a number of trails take backpacking enthusiasts into the spectacular mountain scenery. Rustic wilderness campsites exist along these trails, and for the less energetic a number of less arduous day hikes are also available. Details of these can be found in the literature produced by BC Parks on Tweedsmuir. The park is also popular for horseback riding.

Additional information

With some superb scenery and varied terrain, the South Tweedsmuir area definitely is worthy of more than an overnight stop. The area is a real delight for those who enjoy back-country exploration. Details of all the facilities and activities available can be obtained from the park's headquarters near the Atnarko River campground.

(courtesy BC Parks)

Additional Campgrounds

Ts'il?os

Pronounced "Sigh-loss," this wilderness park is accessed from Highway 20 by taking one of two gravel roads, Tatla Lake road being the only option for those without a four-wheel drive. Two campgrounds are available, providing a total of 32 spaces. Services are very limited and there is neither water nor wood. One popular recreational activity is fishing for lake and rainbow trout and Dolly Varden in the 50-kilometre-long Chilko Lake, which is the largest natural high-elevation freshwater lake in North America. Other activities include hiking and wildlife viewing. A number of private lodges and resorts operate in the area.

Barkerville, well worth the visit. Step back in time
in this restored gold rush town.

8   North by Northwest

The North by Northwest region stretches from the Canadian Rockies to the Pacific Ocean and incorporates mountain ranges, deep valleys, majestic fjords, glaciers, densely forested landscapes, lakes, and rivers. In addition to its natural beauty it is an area rich in First Nations history and culture. The region includes campgrounds situated on the minor roads leading off the Trans-Canada/Yellowhead Highway (Route 16) as well as those on the Highway itself west of McBride all the way to, and including, the Queen Charlotte Islands. This region also encompasses route 37, a gravel and paved road that takes travellers from Kitimat to the road's junction with the Alaska Highway and into the Yukon. The 17 beautiful—sometimes very remote— provincial parks dotted across this area ensure public access to the extraordinary scenery and offer opportunities for wonderful holiday adventures.

Lakelse Lake. (courtesy BC Parks)

Babine Lake

Location

Why not stay on the banks of the longest natural lake in BC? This 177-kilometre-long fishing haven is found after travelling 35 kilometres along a gravel road from a turnoff on route 16, near Burns Lake, which is the nearest settlement offering amenities. Babine Lake is located on the same road as Ethel F. Wilson Provincial Park.

Facilities

There are two camping locations offering a total of 32 campsites situated on the shore of Babine Lake. Facilities are rudimentary and consist of pit toilets, water, wood, picnic benches, and fire pits.

Recreational activities

There is a boat launch, and Babine Lake provides angling opportunities for rainbow trout and char. Because of its somewhat distant location, at Babine Lake campers have an opportunity to see a wide array of wildlife such as moose and bear. Swimming and sailing are additional activities that can be enjoyed at this remote spot.

Additional information

The area is currently being developed and has been known previously as Pendleton Bay. The approach to this campground by a 35-kilometre gravel road combined with the limited facilities available, means that many are dissuaded from staying at Babine Lake. If you can undertake the drive, the scenery and tranquillity are very rewarding. Campers need to be aware that bears frequent the area, and you must ensure all necessary precautions are taken with food (see section 1). The community of Burns Lake, originally called Burnt Lake after a nearby fire, now serves as the major retail source of fishing equipment and supplies. A number of commercial resorts that have been gradually developing in the area offer fishing, canoeing, horseback riding, and skiing excursions. In summary, this spot is ideal for those who want to get away from it all and fish. If you prefer other recreational pursuits, you should try somewhere else.

Beaumont

Location

This provincial park is located on Fraser Lake, west of Vanderhoof, 130 kilometres from Prince George. Early people named the area "Natleh" and used trails in this area to trade with the people of neighbouring settlements. During the last century fur traders used the same trails. The remains of Fort Fraser, which was established by Simon Fraser in 1806, are situated within the park. Food, gas, and accommodation are available just a few kilometres away at Fort Fraser to the west of the park or Fraser Lake to the east.

Facilities

There are 49 large campsites at this location. Some are quite open and exposed while others are situated amongst trees. The park has a sani-station, flush toilets, and facilities for the disabled. A number of campsites are available for reservation.

Recreational activities

A range of recreational activities are available, including swimming in a designated swimming area (a change house is located close to the beach); sunbathing; boating; and fishing for kokanee, char, burbot, rainbow trout, and sturgeon. Boaters should be aware that strong winds can easily transform the generally calm waters of Fraser Lake and cause a serious hazard. There are hiking trails, a children's play area, and horseshoe pits.

Additional information

The campground is surrounded by the Hazelton, Skeena, and Omineca mountains, with trees of willow, poplar, birch, spruce, and aspen making it a very attractive location. The site was originally chosen by early pioneers for its commanding view and because of the breezes which kept mosquitoes at bay. When I visited (late August) there were no signs of the dreaded bug; others, however, may tell a different story. Beaumont is an ideal location to stop for a picnic or take a stroll. The play area and beach make it particularly attractive for parents who have young children to entertain.

Boya Lake

Location

A stunningly beautiful sight awaits the camper who heads for Boya Lake. The lake is remarkable for its clarity and aquamarine colour, the result of light being reflected from the lake bottom, which is comprised of silt and shell fragments. In this regard Boya is quite unlike the lakes found in many other BC provincial parks and a wonderful phenomenon to photograph.

(courtesy BC Parks)

Boya Lake Provincial Park is situated 34 kilometres from the Cassiar-Alaska Highway junction where the nearest services are located. Two kilometres of gravel road lead to the campground itself, which is characterized by truly spectacular views of the Cassiar Mountains and situated adjacent to Boya Lake.

Facilities

The campground has 44 spaces of a variety of shapes and sizes. Some are close to the lake; some are just for tents; most are private and set amongst black and white spruce trees. There is no sani-station and only basic facilities (picnic tables, pit toilets, wood, water, fire pit).

Recreational activities

Because the lake is so clear, fishing in this location is not good, but it is possible to fish for grayling a short distance away in Dease River. There is a small 1½-kilometre lakeside trail from which a wealth of songbirds and waterfowl attracted to the area by its topography, vegetation, and mild climate can be seen. The lake is ideal for boating and (although somewhat cold) also for swimming. Photographers will enjoy the blend of spectacular scenery and plant life.

Additional information

The quietest campsite on route 37, Boya Lake also seems to have been personally cared for. When I visited, a display of 36 photographs of the wildflowers found in the region had been erected alongside the usual park information. In addition, a box where campers could deposit and select reading material had been placed at the entrance. The main draw of this campground must, however, be the crystal-clear lake and stunning views. Boya Lake is a gorgeous location in which to stop.

Ethel F. Wilson Memorial

Location

This small park is named after Ethel Wilson (1888-1980), who wrote the acclaimed novel *Swamp Angel*, about a woman escaping a disastrous marriage by travelling to a remote lake in the north of BC. The park is an ideal spot for those who perhaps may not want to run away from a flawed relationship, but who desire to escape the crowds. Positioned 24 kilometres off Highway 16 along a gravel road, the secluded campground is on the edge of Pinkut Lake. The nearest facilities can be found in Burns Lake, a 30-40 minute drive from the site. Burns Lake is the main service centre for this region known as the Lakes District, which includes over 300 lakes.

Facilities

Ten sites are available in this park, and as is normal in BC Parks' more remote locations, only the basic camping services exist: pit toilets, water, wood, picnic table, and fire pit.

Recreational activities

The area's main activity is fishing for rainbow trout. An informal boat launch is available, and it is possible to swim in the lake. There is a picnic day-use area and excellent opportunities for viewing wildlife such as moose and bear. Salmon spawning channels can be found 30 kilometres northwest of the park on Babine Lake.

Additional information

Burns Lake claims to have 4,828 kilometres of fishing within a 100-kilometre radius of the town. If you are not attracted by this pastime, my advice would be to camp somewhere else. Babine Lake/Pendleton Bay Provincial Park, located a further 11 kilometres along the same road, offers facilities similar to those available at Ethel F. Wilson.

Exchamsiks River

Location

Look out for the extremely rare Kermodei or "white" black bear if planning to camp in the Skeena valley. This exotic, distinct animal is a subspecies of the black bear but its fur ranges from chestnut blond to white. You are more likely to see the image than the real thing, however, as the town of Terrace has the bear's form as its municipal symbol. Exchamsiks River Provincial Park is between Terrace and Prince Rupert, near the merging of the Exchamsiks and Skeena Rivers on the Yellowhead Highway. The nearest services are at Terrace, 55 kilometres away.

Facilities

Twenty campsites exist amongst an old-growth forest of giant Sitka spruce, making it a shady and calming environment in which to camp. The campground has all the basic amenities usually found in BC parks (picnic tables, pit toilets, wood, water, fire pit). There is no sani-station.

Recreational activities

The campground has a boat launch, and fishing for salmon is reputed to be very rewarding. A small self-guided nature trail is also available for park visitors.

Additional information

This provincial park is adjacent to a breathtaking stretch of Highway 16 known as "the valley of the thousand rainbows," so-called because of the weather conditions. A torrential rainstorm one moment can be quickly followed by brilliant sunshine the next, which is something to consider for those whose camping involves sleeping under canvas. Wildlife viewing in this region is very good and can include sightings of fox, deer, coyote, black bear, deer, moose, and the famous kermodei bear.

A "must-read" for visitors travelling between Prince George and Prince Rupert is Dr. R.G. Large's *Skeena, River of Destiny*. A new edition of this BC classic was published in 1996.

Kinaskan Lake

Location

For those who have bounced along the gravel section of Highway 37, Kinaskan Lake is a gift from the gods. Set in the south Stikine Plateau and Iskut River Valley between the Skeena and Coast Mountains is a remote lakeside campground. One hundred and eight kilometres north of the campground is the community of Dease Lake, the "jade capital of the world," which offers a number of amenities such as gas, propane, food, and lodging. More limited amenities are available at Iskut, approximately 40 minutes' drive north from Kinaskan Lake.

Facilities

The campground is situated in a desirable location on the lake itself, and a large number of the 50 campsites are on the water's edge. The sites, which are surrounded by trees and quite large, award more privacy than those of Kinaskan Lake's nearest competitor, Meziadin Lake, three hours drive away. There is no sani-station. Only the basic amenities exist (picnic tables, pit toilets, wood, water, fire pit).

Recreational activities

The lake fishing for rainbow trout here is reputed to be excellent. There is a boat launch, and swimming is possible, although the lake is prone to high winds and waves which often can develop quite suddenly. This is the closest provincial park to Mount Edziza Park, which covers over 230,000 hectares. Mount Edziza Park and recreational area was established to conserve some spectacular volcanic landscapes, including lava flows, cinder fields, and basalt plateaus. The Mowdade Trail leads from Kinaskan Lake to the Coffee Crater area of Mount Edziza Park.

Additional information

Wood is stored under a canopy at this park—a real benefit for those who have to utilize it after wet conditions. This area also offers quite beautiful scenery and is a welcome rest for those who have endured the gravel section of Route 37.

Kleanza Creek

Location

At the turn of the century, the area in which this park is now situated was inhabited by gold seekers. Some years later in 1934, a 180-gram nugget of gold was taken from the creek, and there may be some more gold left. . . . The campground is situated 19 kilometres east of Terrace, where all amenities can be found.

Facilities

The 21 large campsites in Kleanza Creek Provincial Park receive privacy and shade from the tall fir trees. Many sites overlook the clear bubbling waters of the creek itself—a calming sound to lull you to sleep. Facilities are basic, (pit toilets, wood, water, picnic tables, fire pit); there is limited wheelchair access and no sani-station.

Recreational activities

There is an exquisite, relaxing ambiance at this location. Leisure pursuits include a one-kilometre trail leading up to a viewpoint above the creek. There is also a smaller trail that runs alongside the creek. If you look hard, the remains of the Cassia Hydraulic Mining Company's operations can be seen above the canyon. Pink salmon are often observed in the creek during the fall, and there is limited fishing potential.

Additional information

"Kleanza" means "gold" in the Tsimshian people's language. Maybe it is because I visited this park during good weather, but the campground lives in my memory as serene and quite beautiful. Even if you are not intending to stay the night, Kleanza Creek is a perfect place to stop and relax, for BC Parks has conveniently placed benches which look onto the waters tumbling down the creek. The only note of caution is that bears occasionally pass through the area. A highly recommended, exquisite place to camp.

Lakelse Lake

Location

For campers who crave hot springs, this is the place to be. The location of Lakelse Lake Provincial Park just three kilometres from Mount Layton Hot Springs combined with the comprehensive range of facilities the park offers make it a very attractive campsite for all ages. Set amongst majestic old-growth forest and located 24 kilometres south of Terrace on Highway 37, the park provides a beautiful haven for the traveller. Services can be found either in Terrace or in Kitimat, 33 kilometres to the south.

Facilities

Set within a forest of cedar, hemlock, and Sitka spruce are 156 large, well-organized and well-maintained campsites (gravel), catering to every type of recreational vehicle. A full range of facilities exists here, including a sani-station, flush toilets, and showers. Facilities for the disabled are also present and reservations are accepted.

Recreational activities

The lake offers excellent canoeing, sailing, and water-skiing, and there is a paved boat launch. There are beaches, picnic shelters, and a children's playground. A 45-minute interpretive trail that leads through the park allows closer exploration of the old-growth forest, and interpretive programs are offered by BC Parks staff throughout the summer. In the lake and at the nearby Skeena and Kitimat rivers anglers can catch steelhead, rainbow trout, Dolly Varden, and all five species of Pacific Salmon. In August, hundreds of sockeye salmon can be seen in William's Creek at the end of the park. The adjacent Mount Layton Hot Springs Resort has water slides and mineral pools as well as a cafe, restaurant, and pub. The resort offers a $1.00 reduction in admission price to those staying at Lakelse Lake Provincial Park. The town of Kitimat is a 30-minute drive away. Here visitors can undertake a variety of activities, including tours of a salmon hatchery.

Additional information

Lakelse really is a delight to visit for the wide array of activities it provides both within the confines of its boundary and in the larger vicinity. Families with young children will find camping here particularly enjoyable. It is easy to spend an entire day at the hot springs, and children (and some adults) will be entertained for hours on the water slides and in the play areas. The older generation should also appreciate the therapeutic waters of the springs, which are open well into the evening hours. I spent a wonderful Wednesday evening in mid-September being just one of six people enjoying the hot springs, after which we played darts and shuffleboard in the pub over food and drinks. Returning to the uncrowded campground at 10:00 p.m., I was met at the gate by the BC Parks representative ready to collect my camping fee and ensure that I was having a good time (I felt rather like a teenager whose father has waited up for her to return home.) If you get the opportunity, stay at Lakelse. You will not regret it.

Meziadin Lake

Location

Ever seen a live bear trap? When I visited Meziadin Lake a trap was kept at the park, although I was informed by the BC Parks attendant that it had not been used for a while. Meziadin Lake Provincial Park is in the Nass Basin and rewards the visitor with excellent views of the Coast Mountains. As you travel north from Highway 16 this is the first of three provincial park campgrounds on Route 37. It is just south of Meziadin Junction, the turnoff for Stewart, which has a shop, cafe, gas, and tourist information. More extensive services can be found in Stewart, 65 kilometres away.

Facilities

The park has 46 open gravel campsites providing little privacy; a few are situated on the lakeshore. There is no sani-station, and because of the prominence of bears in the area, garbage has to be stored in the only concrete structure on the site. All eating, cooking, and drinking utensils must be kept in a vehicle day and night. There is limited access for the disabled, and facilities are the basic ones found in BC parks (firewood, picnic tables, fire pit, water, and pit toilets).

Recreational activities

Recreational pursuits include fishing for rainbow trout and Dolly Varden in the lake, swimming, and boating. Nearby at the Meziadin River there is a salmon counting fence. The road to Stewart provides a breathtaking excursion from which over 20 glaciers may be viewed, including Bear Glacier, which comes right down to the road itself. Stewart and Hyder are early gold- and silver-mining communities located 65 kilometres from the campground. There are a number of pleasant cafes and restaurants in Stewart itself.

Additional information

This campground seems to be the busiest on route 37 and is a popular place for those interested in fishing. Bears are particularly prevalent during the salmon spawning season. A visit to Hyder at this time provides the best opportunity of seeing both black and grizzly bears in safety. For those who do not want to cook breakfast, the cafe at Meziadin Junction provides a somewhat rudimentary alternative.

(courtesy BC Parks)

Naikoon

Location

Naikoon is a photographer's paradise where the atmospheric conditions coupled with the variety of plants and wildlife combine to yield fantastic photographic opportunities. The only provincial park with camping facilities on the Queen Charlotte Islands, Naikoon is found on Graham Island, the most northerly of the Charlottes. "Naikoon" means "long nose" and is derived

from the Haida name "Nai-kun." There are two campground facilities: Misty Meadows, is located near Tlell, 42 kilometres north of Skidegate on Highway 16; Agate Beach, is 26 kilometres northeast of Masset on a secondary road. Services are available in the communities of Port Clements, Tlell, Masset, and Queen Charlotte City.

(courtesy BC Parks)

Facilities

The 21 sites at Agate Beach are close to the ocean and somewhat exposed; in contrast, the 30 at Misty Meadow are situated under pine trees. Neither have sani-stations or flush toilets. There is limited access for the disabled at Agate Beach. Wilderness camping is permitted throughout the park, and three wilderness shelters are located along East Beach near the mouths of the Cape Ball and Oeanda Rivers and at Fife Point.

Recreational activities

Numerous recreational activities can be enjoyed at this park, where visitors frequently spend a week or more. Trail details can be obtained from reading the park information leaflet available from the information board at the campground entrance. There are over 60 kilometres of beach to explore, and it is possible to dig for clams and swim. Coho salmon and steelhead can be caught in the Tlell river, while opportunities to see a vast array of wildlife abound. The Tow Hill Ecological Reserve and Rose Spit Ecological Reserve have been established in the park to protect the flora and fauna. It is illegal to camp, fish, hunt, or use motorized vehicles in these ecological reserves.

Additional information

The Queen Charlottes, renowned for overcast skies and frequent fogs, are often referred to as "the misty islands." Campers should come well prepared for cold, damp conditions, even if you plan to visit in July and stay in a vehicle. If you wear the correct gear, you can enjoy walking along deserted, windswept beaches, and there are excellent opportunities to see a wide assortment of sea mammals and birds—the Charlottes boast the second highest eagle nest density in the world.

Paarens Beach

Location

Watch the sun go down and the stars come out from this lovely campground on the warm southern shores of Stuart Lake. Paarens Beach Provincial Park is situated on one of the largest lakes in the province amidst the Nechako Plateau Hills, a little under two hours from Prince George on Highway 27. Approximately 15 minutes away by car is the historic town of Fort Saint James, which has all amenities.

Facilities

The campground contains 36 sites of which six are close to the water's edge. With a few exceptions the sites are large, private, and partly wooded. There is a sani-station and pit toilets. A number of campsites are available for reservation.

Recreational activities

For those with young children or for those who enjoy fishing and water sports, there is a great deal to do in the park itself. The site boasts a large sandy beach, and BC Parks have made the location ideal for families by providing a change house, picnic tables, and a picnic shelter. Fishing includes rainbow trout and lake char, and there is a concrete boat launch. Stuart Lake is also an ideal location for sailing and windsurfing, but users must be cautious because of the sudden strong winds that can easily develop on this large lake. The National Historic Park at Fort Saint James provides an account of pioneer life in the reconstructed Hudson's Bay Trading Post and is well worth a visit. Here there is an informative interpretive program where guides dressed in period costume give accounts and anecdotes of the lives of the early settlers. For the more energetic, the Mount Pope trail just north of the community takes hikers on a two- to four-hour hike (one way) up to the top of Mount Pope, where there are spectacular views of Stuart Lake.

Additional information

Swimmer's itch can be a problem here at certain times of the year. The site is very close to Sowchea Bay, where there are comparable facilities, and it is easy to travel between the two to determine which provides the best camping location for your needs.

Prudhomme Lake

Location

Twenty kilometres east of Prince Rupert is the small forested campground of Prudhomme Lake. Access from Highway 16 is immediate, and all amenities are available in Prince Rupert. By staying here, campers can enjoy the best of two provincial parks. Diane Lake Provincial Park is just one kilometre away.

Facilities

Prudhomme Lake Provincial Park offers 24 spacious campsites adjacent to the lakefront. There is no sani-station or access for the disabled, and facilities are basic (picnic tables, pit toilets, wood, water, fire pit).

Recreational activities

While the activities at Prudhomme Lake are limited to fishing for steelhead, rainbow trout, and Dolly Varden, Diane Lake has a day-use area for swimming, canoeing, and sunbathing. From Diane Lake Park it is possible to take a trail that meanders through the coastal rain forest to Diane Creek Falls, or to fish in the creeks which run through the park. Prudhomme Lake provides the nearest provincial park camping to the town of Prince Rupert. There you can find many leisure activities, including the Museum of Northern BC, a railway museum, a self-guided walking tour, and an 18-hole golf course. In the adjacent community of Port Edward it is possible to visit the restoration of one of the oldest fishing canneries on the BC coast and to learn of the development of commercial fishing in this area.

Additional information

In August and September it is possible to see salmon spawning in Diane Creek, and black-tailed deer also inhabit this area. From Prince Rupert, air charters to the Khutzeymateen, 45 kilometres north of the city, can be arranged. This area of 445 square kilometres is home to the largest known grizzly bear population on the BC coast and one of the largest in the world.

Purden Lake

Location

Exceptional photographic opportunities can be had at Purden Lake, especially in the early morning as the mist slowly clears over the calm waters of the lake. Situated in the foothills of the Rockies, less than an hour's drive from Prince George on a paved road two kilometres off the Yellowhead Highway, is this popular campground regularly used by Prince George residents and visitors to the region. Services such as gas, propane, and restaurants are conveniently located less than five kilometres from the campground itself, although its proximity to Prince George means that with motorized transport, campers are within an hour's reach of every need.

Facilities

There are 78 campsites set amongst trees, a sani-station but no showers or flush toilets. All sites are relatively private, and some sites are specifically set aside for tents. Facilities for the handicapped are available.

Recreational activities

Amenities in the park include an adventure playground, horseshoe pit, a sandy beach and swimming area. Lakeside walking trails award beautiful views of the surrounding area and make it possible to explore a variety of plant life. There is a concrete boat launch and water-skiing is permitted on the lake. Anglers can fish for rainbow trout and burbot. The city of Prince George provides a wealth of things to see and do, including the Fraser-Fort George Regional Museum and the new University of Northern British Columbia, which affords spectacular views of the surrounding landscape.

Additional information

With its beautiful setting amidst undulating forested mountains and yet within easy access to Prince George, Purden Lake is one of the region's most popular parks. Consequently it is regularly full at weekends, and in 1997 reservations were not taken. The lakeside is very picturesque and can be quite haunting, especially in the early morning as the mist clears over the water.

(courtesy BC Parks)

157

Red Bluff

Location
Like Babine Lake Provincial Park, Red Bluff is situated on Babine Lake, the longest natural freshwater lake in British Columbia. So-called because of the dramatic reddish cliffs under which it nestles, the park is a few kilometres south of the community of Granisle, a 45-minute drive on paved road from Highway 16.

Facilities
The provincial park has 27 large sites set in woodland; a few overlook the lake while a few are more open and closer to the day-use area. There is an overflow camping area but no sani-station or flush toilets, and facilities are the basic ones generally found in BC Parks (firewood, picnic tables, fire pit, water, and pit toilets).

Recreational activities
Visitors to the park can engage in a number of pursuits including fishing (literature from BC Parks boasts that cutthroat trout up to one kilogram, rainbow trout up to six kilograms, and char up to thirteen kilograms can be caught here), boating, swimming, and hiking. A number of small trails provide the opportunity to see wildlife—black bear and moose being particularly abundant—and one trail overlooks the marsh area where patience can be rewarded by a sighting of elusive birds and waterfowl. The Fulton River Salmon Hatchery just south of the park also deserves a visit for the opportunities it provides to view salmon leaping up a series of channels and to learn about the salmon spawning process.

Additional information
This area is known for its wildlife, and animals are regularly sighted along the quiet drive from Highway 16 to the park. The lake can become extremely rough, as high winds are easily whipped up in the area. I spent a somewhat uneasy night at this campground listening to the winds high in the trees and wondering which tree was going to crash down on top of me. My fears were totally unfounded. Granisle, which was a copper-mining town until the mine closed in 1992, appears to have little to commend it.

Seeley Lake

Location

Remember to bring your binoculars as you will be rewarded with sightings of bald eagles, ospreys, and kingfishers together with a variety of waterfowl. Nestled amongst the Hazelton Mountains and located on Highway 16 just west of New Hazelton, where services are located, is Seeley Lake, a quaint and quite picturesque campground.

Facilities

The campground itself is relatively small, containing only 20 sites, all of which are large, private, and wooded. Approximately half the sites overlook the lake. There is no sani-station, and only the basic facilities offered by BC Parks exist (pit toilets, wood, water, fire pit, picnic tables).

Recreational activities

The fish that can be caught here include cutthroat and rainbow trout. Swimming is possible although there is no beach. Seeley Lake is only a short drive from Old Hazelton, where K'San has created an authentic reproduction of a Gitksan Indian village, including six longhouses with painted fronts and totem poles, a gift shop, and a carving school. In the summer K'San dancers perform in the early evenings. For those interested in exploring First Nations culture this campground is also an ideal base from which to travel to see the totem poles of Kispioux, Kitwanga, and Kitwancool.

Additional information

I stopped here early one morning as the mist was rising over the lake and the surrounding snow-topped mountains were just coming into view; the moment was quite magical. The only disadvantage to the location is that the campsites are quite near the road; light sleepers may want earplugs. Seeley Lake makes a lovely picnic spot for those who do not have the time to camp. Visitors to Hazelton will enjoy Dr. Eldon Lee's *A Western Doctor's Odyssey* describing his medical years here as a rural doctor.

K'san Village. (courtesy The BC Adventure Network)

Sowchea Bay

Location

This region is full of historical accounts of early European settlers and provides an informative and relaxing recreational destination. Sowecha Bay is five minutes' drive from Paarens Beach Provincial Park beside the same large lake (Stuart), 70 kilometres from the Yellowhead Highway. Its location and the recreational facilities it provides are very similar to those available at Paarens Beach. Campers can easily travel between the two to decide which campground to choose. The nearest community is Fort Saint James.

Facilities

This a particularly attractive campground with 30 campsites available. The advantage Sowchea Bay has over its nearby neighbour, Paarens Beach, is that all sites here are located on the water's edge. The sites are quite large, relatively private, and set amongst trees. There is no sani-station. Unlike Paarens Beach, Sowchea Bay campground does not accept reservations.

Recreational activities

Recreational activities are similar to Paarens Beach (except there are no day-use picnic facilities). These activities include fishing for rainbow trout, lake char, burbot, and kokanee in Stuart Lake; swimming; sunbathing; sailing and boating (there is a boat launch at the site). In addition, the nearby community of Fort Saint James provides historical interest, or for those who prefer, a nine-hole golf course with views of Stuart Lake.

Additional information

Although Paarens Beach seems to be the more popular site, perhaps because it has a day-use area and accepts reservations, I prefer Sowchea Bay. With all sites on the beach it is an ideal place to watch the sun set while taking a stroll along the shoreline. The views are quite spectacular and on a clear night the star-gazing from this vantage point is awe-inspiring. Caution must be exercised by those who plan to windsurf or sail on the waters of the lake, which is prone to high winds and waves.

Stuart Lake from Sowchea Bay Provincial Park.

Tyhee Lake

Location

Children adore Tyhee Lake for the beach; anglers love it for the fish; bird-watchers are attracted to the abundant bird life; but for me, Tyhee Lake's biggest attraction is the friendly atmosphere it conveys. While it is the convention in BC parks to say hello and pass the time of day with other campers, when I stayed at Tyhee everyone I met was happy and communicative. Consequently Tyhee Lake lives in my memory as being the "very friendly provincial park." This family-oriented campground is a 15-minute drive east of Smithers on Highway 16 near the quaint settlement of Telkwa. All amenities are therefore available within a few kilometres of the park itself.

Facilities

This is a large and well-maintained campground set amidst an aspen forest on the side of Tyhee (Maclure) Lake. There are 59 campsites—a few with views over the lake—accommodating every kind of recreational vehicle as well as tents. In addition to all the normal facilities found in a provincial park Tyhee Lake has a sani-station, flush toilets, and showers, making it one of the more expensive parks in which to stay. Reservations are accepted.

Recreational activities

A beautiful beach provides access for swimming, there is a boat launch, and water-skiing is permitted on the lake. Horseshoes and volleyball are also available as is a play area for children. Fish found in the lake include cutthroat and stocked rainbow trout. An interpretive trail has been developed around the campground, and there is a marsh-viewing platform where it is possible to see loons, rednecked grebes, ruffed grouse, and beaver. Throughout the summer, BC Parks provides a range of activities in the amphitheatre. In addition, the communities of Smithers and Telkwa are pleasant places to visit. Smithers houses a wildlife museum that displays a variety of big game animals, and Telkwa has a history dating back to the 1860s.

Additional information

The large, well-kept, day-use area and the park's proximity to the Yellowhead Highway make this an ideal picnic spot if you do not have time to spend the night. However, the many activities available coupled with the availability of showers means that Tyhee Lake is the perfect place for family camping and consequently a location where many visitors spend more than one night.

9   Peace River Alaska Highway

Famous for excellent fishing and big game and set between the foothills of the Rocky Mountains to the west and the plains of Alberta to the east, this remote northern part of British Columbia provides wide-open spaces, mountains, rivers, and valleys. The area incorporates Highway 97 north of Prince George all the way to Dawson Creek and beyond, forming the Alaska Highway up to the Yukon border. While there are not a lot of large settlements along this route, excellent wildlife viewing opportunities compensate for the lack of people, and travellers are blessed with an open road. Even at the peak of summer it is not unusual to drive for thirty minutes without seeing another vehicle. Region 9 also includes Highway 29 from Fort Saint John to Tumbler Ridge and Highway 2 and the eastern section of Highway 1. Go—travel and enjoy a region of BC that feels like it has been created with only you in mind.

Beatton

Location

For the angler, Beatton Provincial Park boasts the best fishing for walleye in British Columbia. For those who do not fish, Beatton provides a lovely camping retreat that has been enjoyed by campers for decades. Established on 14 September 1934, this is one of BC's oldest provincial parks. Beatton is located 13 kilometres northwest of Fort Saint John off Highway 97 on a paved road access. Limited services can be found on Highway 97 while a more comprehensive range are available at Fort Saint John.

Facilities

Thirty-seven campsites are found here on the eastern side of Charlie Lake set among poplar and spruce trees. Some spots are on the lakeside; all are large and very private. There is no sani-station, and facilities are restricted to the basic ones found in BC Parks (fire pit, wood, water, pit toilets, picnic tables). The park is wheelchair accessible and reservations are accepted.

Recreational activities

Aspen-lined trails lead from the campground to a 300-metre beach on the banks of Charlie Lake. While it is possible to swim, the high algae content of the lake may make it unappealing. There is good fishing for northern pike and walleye. A boat launch is available, and hikers will enjoy the fifteen kilometres of walking trails. In addition to over 40 species of birds and waterfowl, moose, mule, and white-tailed deer can be seen in the park. Beatton Provincial Park also has an adventure playground, horseshoes, and a baseball field.

Additional information

The 440-hectare park is popular in both summer and winter. BC Parks produces literature on the winter recreational pursuits available at Beatton. During the colder months, visitors can go tobogganing, cross-country skiing, ice fishing for walleye and northern pike, or snowshoeing. The park provides "warm up huts" (for someone from the south of the province these conjure up wonderful images). Wood is stored under a canopy in this park—a blessing on a wet day. The site is relatively close to Charlie Lake, and while both offer similar facilities, my preference would be to stay at Beatton.

Buckinghorse River

Location

Buckinghorse River campground is very much oriented toward overnighters travelling the Alaska Highway. When I stayed, I recognized a number of vehicles that I had passed or that had passed me during the course of the day. The campground is located 200 kilometres northwest of Fort Saint John at Mile 173 of the Highway. A restaurant and gas station are conveniently situated adjacent to the campground.

Facilities

Accommodation takes the form of 33 spots, all with a view of the river. They are quite closely positioned with no interspersed vegetation and have little privacy; the better ones are towards the end of the campground. Because the campsite is set a short distance away from the highway, noise is not a problem. All the basic amenities are provided (fire pit, wood, water, pit toilets, picnic tables).

Recreational activities

This campground is primarily for travellers en route to other destinations, so there are limited recreational activities. The river provides an opportunity to fish for arctic grayling, and by taking a short walk downstream it is possible to find areas to swim. As is the case in many provincial parks in the north, it is possible to spend hours star-gazing. The sky seems bigger in this area of the world. Peaceful evenings with only the noise of flowing waters and a crackling fire provide the ideal setting for this astronomical pursuit.

Additional information

BC Parks warns that both black bears and grizzly bears inhabit the area. Caution must be exercised. During the winter months, moose graze here. For those who do not wish to cook their own breakfast or dinner there is a restaurant conveniently located across the road from the campground. Although the camping spots are close to each other, when I stayed (early September) there were only ten spots taken, so it did not feel crowded. Buckinghorse River is one of the better functional roadside campgrounds.

Carp Lake

Location
Why not camp on top of the world? At an elevation of 841 metres, Carp Lake is a picturesque island-dotted lake covering 19,000 hectares of the Nechako Plateau. It can be reached by turning off Highway 97 at McLeod Lake (where the nearest services can be found) and travelling along a gravel road for 32 kilometres. This gravel road is single lane and not particularly good in places. There are a number of tight corners, and BC Parks information cautions the route is not suitable for cars or trailers during the spring break-up period.

Facilities
Visitors do not yearn for something to do here. Patrons can choose between two campgrounds. The main one, Carp Lake, is situated at Kettle Bay and has 90 large sites that can accommodate most recreational vehicles. War Lake campground at the east end of War Lake has just 12 sites, and these are not suitable for larger vehicles. Wilderness camping is possible on three of the islands in Carp Lake. There is a sani-station, no wheelchair access, and the facilities are the basic ones found in parks of this type (fire pit, wood, water, pit toilets, picnic tables).

Recreational activities
Two sandy beaches are located along the beach trail a 20- and 40-minute walk from the main campground. A boat launch is available, and powerboating and canoeing can be enjoyed on the lake. Fishing is good. Rainbow trout, burbot, and northern squawfish are plentiful in the lake, while a short trail leading to McLeod River takes anglers to an ideal fly fishing spot. A number of trails exist in the park for those who wish to hike or mountain bike. One of these trails follows a section of a route used long ago by the Carrier Indians between Fort McLeod and Fort Stewart. Wildlife viewing is good, and moose are often seen at the lake, especially at dawn and dusk.

Additional information
In his journal of 1806 Simon Fraser wrote of the Carrier Indians who visited the area to catch large quantities of fish similar to carp. The park is still a magnet for those who enjoy fishing. The summertime temperature at Carp Lake can be cool, averaging 12–18 degrees in July, and can drop considerably at night, so make sure you bring enough warm clothing.

Charlie Lake

Location

Naturalists love this area for the chance of seeing a wide variety of wildlife, including white-tail and mule deer, black bear, beaver, moose, and an array of waterfowl. It is easy to see why this campground situated on the southwestern shore of Charlie Lake in the broad valley of the Peace River is popular with both locals and visitors. It is conveniently discovered 11 kilometres north of Fort Saint John on the Alaska Highway at it's junction with Highway 29. All services can be found at Fort Saint John while more limited facilities are available closer to the campground on Highway 97.

Facilities

The 58-site campground is set amongst a heavily treed deciduous forest of aspen, birch, alder, lodgepole pine, and spruce. While a few sites are located close to the road, most are not. The sites are large, well-appointed, and suitable for every type of recreational vehicle. Some have grassed areas for tents. The park is wheelchair accessible, has a sani-station, and accepts reservations.

Recreational activities

Fishing in summer and winter is a popular activity here; northern pike and walleye inhabit the lake. Literature from BC Parks states Charlie Lake is the walleye "hot spot" of the province (what a claim to fame!). A two-kilometre trail leads from the campground to the lake, where there is a boat launch and from where it is possible to swim, although the high algae content of the lake may put you off. The campground has a play area for children and a horseshoe pit. For those who choose activities away from the campground, an 18-hole golf course and country club can be found at Mile 54 of the Alaska Highway.

Additional information

Archaeological research in the area has revealed aboriginal habitation dating back 10,000 years. If you succeed in obtaining a campsite away from the road, Charlie Lake is a delightful place to camp. Depending on the time of year, a variety of berries grow in the vicinity, but remember, picking the vegetation in BC parks is prohibited.

Crooked River

Location
There are two kinds of campgrounds: those geared for overnight camping and those where you want to spend time relaxing and overdosing on BC's wonderful scenery. Crooked River falls into the second category. This delightful spot is found in the Fraser Basin amongst a forest of lodgepole pine with alder, birch, aspen, and spruce. It is situated 80 kilometres north of Prince George on Highway 97. The nearby community of Bear Lake provides accommodation, gas, and food.

Facilities
There are ninety spots of various sizes here. A tarmac approach road gives way to a gravel road upon entering the camping area. As with all BC provincial park campgrounds, details at the entrance to the park illustrate where the largest sites are and where the pull-throughs are located. Some sites overlook the lake, and trees provide privacy and shade. There is a sani-station as well as flush and pit toilets but no showers. The campground is accessible by wheelchair, and reservations are accepted.

Recreational activities
The park is on Bear Lake, which has a good sandy beach ideal for children. Youngsters will also enjoy the adventure playground, volleyball, and horseshoe pits. Fishing is not confined to Bear Lake. Nearby, Squaw and Hart Lakes and the river yield opportunities to catch rainbow and brook trout, Dolly Varden, arctic grayling, and whitefish. There are a number of trails that take about an hour to complete as well as longer hikes. The Crooked River trail follows the same route early Canadian explorers such as Simon Fraser and Alexander Mackenzie took in the 19th century. It is possible to canoe and kayak, and with powerboats prohibited, paddlers are ensured of a tranquil visit. Ornithologists can be rewarded by sightings of bald eagles and ospreys.

Additional information
BC Parks literature states that Crooked River was originally established to protect the area's attractive lakes and surrounding landscape. I stayed at this location in June one year and got completely bitten from head to toe by mosquitoes, despite the fact I dressed in layers of clothing and stood over the fire pit. This experience tainted my opinion of the park, although I have not had the same problem on subsequent visits. Crooked River is a beautifully maintained campground which can be perfect if you choose a mosquito-free time.

Gwillim Lake

Location

Gwillim Lake is definitely a place to include on your camping itinerary. It is found in a stunning location amongst the Rocky Mountain foothills, with breathtaking mountain views, at an elevation of 765 metres and with 25 kilometres of shoreline. The park is located on Highway 29, a 40-minute drive from Chetwynd to the north and Tumbler Ridge to the south. Services are available in both these centres.

Facilities

All the basic facilities found within BC parks are available at this 49-space park (fire pit, wood, water, pit toilets, picnic tables), which is partially wheelchair accessible. The campsites are located in a lightly pine-forested area; many have commanding views of the lake and Rocky Mountains. There are also a number of walk-in camping spots. No sani-station is provided.

Recreational activities

A perfectly wonderful time can be had here just reading, relaxing, and enjoying the beauty of BC. Other leisure pursuits include fishing for a variety of fish. Arctic grayling, northern pike, Dolly Varden, burbot, and mountain whitefish can be caught, although anglers should be cautioned the deep blue waters of the lake do not yield fantastic fish populations. Gwillim Lake has a boat launch and hiking trails, and the area is very good for observing wildlife, particularly deer and moose, which are most often spotted in the early morning.

Additional information

This park provides some panoramic views of the Rocky Mountains. Above the northwestern shore, an open meadow creates a viewpoint of the western part of the lake. The park is beautiful to visit in the fall when the colours are spectacular, but it really is a gem of a location to visit any time of the year. The town of Chetwynd is basically a forestry community with a relatively small population (3,000), yet it boasts a museum, railway museum, and trapper's cabin—all open to the public. The town also displays a number of interesting chainsaw sculptures by BC artists.

Kiskatinaw

Location

Kiskatinaw is located on the old Alaska Highway. Nearby, aromatic cottonwood trees on the edge of the river exude a delicate perfume in the summer. Primarily used as an overnight camping spot, this 58-hectare provincial park is located on the northern Great Plains, 34 kilometres north of Dawson Creek. Access is achieved by taking a five-kilometre paved road to the campground. Services can be found at Dawson Creek to the south or Taylor to the north.

Facilities

The camping facilities here are basic and include 28 spots secluded in groves of poplar and spruce. Pit toilets, water, firewood, fire pits, and picnic tables are all provided. There is no sani-station or access for the disabled.

Recreational activities

From the campground it is possible to walk to the scenic deep-walled canyon of the Kiskatinaw River and to view the historic curved wooden bridge that was developed for the original Alaska Highway in 1942. An archaeological site is located in the park.

Additional information

The town of Dawson Creek was established in 1931 when the Northern Alberta Railway Line was extended to the area. It flourished in 1942 when American soldiers and engineers arrived to build the Alaska Highway. Dawson Creek is now home to the Mile Zero Post, a three-metre-high marker noting mile zero of the Alaska Highway. The Dawson Creek Station Museum gives information on the construction of this famous road. Many tourists visit Dawson Creek to have their photograph taken at Mile Zero before heading north to the Yukon and Alaska.

Liard River Hot Springs

Location

For any BC Parks enthusiast Liard River Hot Springs must be one of the biggest jewels in the crown. It certainly ranks as one of the top BC Parks for me. The only disadvantage this beautiful park has is that it is the most northerly in BC and therefore not easily accessible to most of the people in the province. Those that do travel this far on the Alaska Highway will be amply rewarded in their efforts. Liard River Hot Springs is situated at Mile 496 of the Highway, 20 kilometres north of Muncho Lake, and is the second largest hot springs in Canada (after Banff). A restaurant and small shop are located across the road from the park itself; more comprehensive services can be found at Muncho Lake.

Alpha Pool at Liard River Hot Springs.

Facilities

At Liard Hot Springs there are 53 large, well appointed, totally private campsites set among trees and suitable for every type of recreational vehicle. There is no sani-station, and the park is wheelchair accessible. Facilities are restricted to the basic ones (fire pit, wood, water, pit toilets, picnic tables). Reservations are accepted. There are no showers . . . but here they aren't needed!

Recreational activities

The biggest attraction to this park is, of course, the hot springs, which have been beautifully maintained in their natural setting. A boardwalk takes campers from the campground to two bathing pools, one an eight- and the other a twelve-minute walk from the campground. Both have change room facilities. At the larger Alpha pool bathers can choose which area of the water to sit in and which temperature to endure (from an almost unbearable 53 degrees where the waters emerge, to a far more comfortable heat). The smaller Beta circular pool is a constant temperature (approximately 42 degrees). It is possible to swim here. In addition to these two mineral pools, a variety of fauna and flora unique to the area can be seen. Over 250 species of boreal forest plants grow in the area and more than 100 bird species visit the park. (Moose and black bear also inhabit the area.) A hanging garden at certain times of the year demonstrates this vegetation which is loved by photographers. BC Parks offers interpretive programs in the summer, and there is a children's play area and horseshoes.

Additional information

The hot springs have been enjoyed by travellers for centuries. Many hundreds of years ago the Kaska Indians bathed here while in 1835 the waters were recorded by Robert Campbell, a Hudson's Bay Company Factor. In 1942, the American Army stationed in the area to build the Alaska Highway constructed the first boardwalk to the pools. I have extremely affectionate memories of the one time I was lucky enough to stay here. We went to the hot pools at 7:00 a.m., before most people were up. A thunderstorm was passing, and we sat in the hot waters watching the lightning as the cold rain fell into the warm pools. After the therapeutic experience, we took our clean, glowing bodies for breakfast in the funky little restaurant across the road from the campground. A perfect start to the day. Liard River Hot Springs is well worth a visit, and unlike many of the commercially developed hot springs in the south of the province, it remains in a totally natural environment. This is one of my favourite provincial parks—if you get a chance, do not wait—GO!

Moberly Lake

Location

This campground is well maintained and a real delight to stay in, but at certain times of the year watch out for black bears who feed on the abundant berries growing in the area. Positioned in the valley of the Moberly River on the south shore of the lake, between the foothills of the Rocky Mountains and the northern Great Plains, Moberly Lake Provincial Park is reached by turning off Highway 29, 24 kilometres northeast of Chetwynd, and taking a good gravel road three kilometres. All services are available at Chetwynd with more limited ones available at Moberly Lake, 11 kilometres from the campground.

Facilities

One hundred and nine large, private camping spots set in a forest of mature white spruce and aspen make this a desirable destination. Streams flow through the campground itself and a few sites overlook the lake. Grassy sites are available and there is ample space for the longest RV. The park is accessible for the disabled. There is a sani-station and reservations are accepted.

Recreational activities

A number of activities can be undertaken both within the park itself and in the wider area. The park has a boat launch, and it is possible to fish for Dolly Varden, whitefish, and char. A developed beach and changing facilities make swimming a delight. There are a number of walks and trails. A children's play area has been built near the lake. A wealth of bird life can be observed in the area, including bald eagles, American kestrels, belted kingfishers, and common loons. In addition, two power dams are easily accessible. The W. A. C. Bennett Dam, one of the largest earth-filled dams in the world, houses a visitor centre with interpretive programs and restaurant, and Peace Canyon Dam is also well worth a visit. Golfing is available nearby.

Additional information

Moberly Lake was named after Henry Moberly, a trader and trapper working for the Hudson's Bay Company, who settled on the shores of the lake in the mid-1800s.

Monkman

Location
Monkman Provincial Park is a wonderland of waterfalls and scenic lakes surrounded by the Hart Ranges of the central Rocky Mountains. Access to this scenery may deter some visitors as it is found after travelling 60 kilometres from Tumbler Ridge on a gravel road. Services are located at Tumbler Ridge.

Facilities
Forty-two camping spots are found here, a number of them less than 50 metres from Murray River. All accommodate every type of recreational vehicle and some have specific areas for tents. Back-country campsites are also available. In addition to the basic facilities (wood, water, picnic tables, pit toilets, fire pit) the park is wheelchair accessible.

Recreational activities
One of the biggest attractions here is undoubtedly the hiking trails. A short trail leads to the spectacular 60-metre Kinuseo Falls, where a viewing platform ensures excellent photographic opportunities. A seven-kilometre (one way) trail leads to the Murray River, where a suspension bridge can be crossed, taking hikers along the Mount Head Trail into the park's back country. This route follows the original one of the Monkman Pass Highway (see below). Powerboats can be launched on the Pine and Murray Rivers, and below the Falls the Murray River can be canoed. Fishing in the lakes and rivers yields trout, char, grayling, and whitefish.

Additional information
In 1922, Alex Monkman, a fur trader, farmer, and visionary, dreamed of creating a route to link the farms of the Peace River to Hensard (northeast of Prince George). In 1936 he formed the Monkham Pass Highway Association, and a year later work started. Unfortunately the project was plagued by lack of funds, and in 1939 with the outbreak of the Second World War, all work ceased. Today, the Monkman Lake Trail follows much of the original highway while the pass bears the name of the pioneer whose dream was never realized.

Muncho Lake

Location

When travelling to or from Muncho Lake, stop near kilometre 760 (mile 474) of the Alaska Highway and look for stone sheep licking the mineral rocks. The best time for viewing is at dawn or dusk in the late spring and early fall. Muncho Lake is an area of parkland covering over 200,000 hectares among the Terminal and Muskwa Ranges of the Rocky Mountains, an area noted not only for its wildlife but also for its classic Rocky Mountain features such as folded and vaulted rock and alluvial fans. Like many provincial parks along the route, it owes its existence to the Alaska Highway and is situated at Mile 422 of the Alaska Highway 250 kilometres west of Fort Nelson. Services such as gas, restaurants, and small shops are located, quite unusually, in the park itself at Muncho Lake.

Facilities

Thirty campsites are positioned in two campgrounds both on the shores of Muncho Lake. The more northerly campground, MacDonald, has 15 spots which are quite close to the road and provide little privacy. Strawberry Flats (my preference) is the more southerly location with 15 spots that are more private, some being on the waterfront. There is no sani-station and facilities are basic in both campgrounds (fire pit, wood, water, pit toilets, picnic tables).

Recreational activities

Muncho Lake, 12 kilometres long and over two kilometres wide in places, enjoys typical Canadian Rocky Mountain scenery and endless photo opportunities. From here, campers can take hiking trails, go boating (there is a boat launch at MacDonald campground) and fish for trout, arctic grayling, Dolly Varden, and whitefish. The park is also noted for its wildlife viewing, including black bears, stone sheep, mountain goats, caribou, deer, and wolf. Average summer lake temperature of the lake, it is not a popular swimming location.

Additional information

Muncho Lake takes its name from native Kaskan Indian meaning "big lake." The jade green colour is derived from copper oxides leached in from the surrounding bedrock coupled with the refraction of sunlight on sediments brought into the lake by glacial melt water. While the scenery here is quite spectacular, the camping can become quite cool and windy.

(courtesy BC Parks)

115 Creek

Location
This area is excellent for wildlife; when I stopped, there were seven caribou and a moose grazing near the campground. In driving down this section of the Alaska Highway, you should expect to make numerous stops and starts to take photographs and identify animals. This 51-hectare wayside campground is situated at Mile 385 of the Alaska Highway at the junction of 115 Creek and MacDonald Creek. Services can be found at Muncho Lake, a 20-minute drive away.

Facilities
There are eight campsites here close to the stream and to the road, very tightly packed and with no privacy. Only the basic facilities exist (fire pit, wood, water, pit toilets, picnic tables).

Recreational activities
This is very much a roadside campground primarily for overnight stops. A small trail leads from the campground to the water's edge where it is possible to view beaver dams and ponds. As mentioned above, there are fantastic opportunities for wildlife viewing.

Additional information
As this provincial park is close to Muncho Lake, where the facilities and scenery are superior, my advice would be to travel on to that campground if you can.

Muncho Lake.

One Island

Location

I have not had the opportunity to visit this park, but without exception, the people I have spoken to who know the area and the literature on the park have all stressed the cleanliness of the lake's water. Somewhat off the beaten track, this 62-hectare provincial park does not have the advantage of being a conveniently situated "roadside" campground for one night's stop, but it will guarantee a very quiet night's rest. One Island Lake Provincial Park is situated 72 kilometres south of Dawson Creek in the foothills of the Rockies. Turn off Highway 2 at Tupper, where services are available, and take an unpaved road 33 kilometres to the campground.

Facilities

There are 30 campsites available on the southeastern shore of the lake, some overlooking the lake itself. Services are limited to the basic ones found in provincial parks (wood, water, fire pit, picnic table, pit toilets).

Recreational activities

It is possible to swim, fish, and boat from this campground. There is a boat launch, and the fishing for rainbow and brook trout is reputed to be excellent with fish reaching over two kilograms in size. The lake is stocked annually. This area is popular with residents of Dawson Creek in both winter and summer.

Additional information

The first settlers of Tupper were a group of Sudetens (Czechoslovakians from the Czech/Polish border) who wanted to escape Hitler and who settled here in the 1930s. For those who do not like travelling on gravel roads, Swan Lake offers a nearby alternative.

Prophet River

Location

According to information published by BC Parks, a spring that surfaces in the park's boundary is "great on hot summer days." I spent a couple of hours trying to locate this spring but could not find it. This 115-hectare park is situated on the banks of Prophet River and is primarily visited by those travelling the Alaska Highway. It is approximately 125 kilometres south of Fort Nelson off Highway 97 at Mile 217. A full range of services can be found at Fort Nelson.

Facilities

There are 45 camping spaces, set in lines with little privacy, although large grassy areas are available on which to pitch tents. The facilities are confined to the basic ones found within BC Parks (fire pit, wood, water, pit toilets, picnic tables).

Recreational activities

Like a number of campgrounds on major roads, this location is essentially utilized by travellers en route to another destination, and therefore few recreational activities are offered. It is possible to hike down to the river, but when I visited, the banks at the water's edge were rapidly being eroded and the trail was not great. The area is also good for observing song and other birds. Wood warblers nest in the surrounding poplar trees, and a collection of ducks and water fowl inhabit the pools by the river.

Additional information

The original Alaska Highway runs through Prophet River Provincial Park. The area has seen considerable economic change during this century. In the 1920s, fur trading was the primary industry; in 1942, 2,000 American troops worked to construct the highway; today, oil and lumber are the main revenue producers, and evidence of these resource industries can be seen when driving between Fort Nelson and Fort St. John.

Stone Mountain

Location

High amongst the breathtaking Rocky Mountain scenery at Mile 373 of the Alaska Highway, 130 kilometres from Fort Nelson, is the Stone Mountain Provincial Park. This campground may be regarded as either bleak or beautiful, depending on the weather and your own personal camping preferences. Full services are available at Fort Nelson, while gas and food can be obtained a few kilometres from the park.

Facilities

Stone Mountain campground is situated at the end of Summit Lake. The 28 campsites are very exposed and close to the road. They all overlook the lake to varying degrees but have little privacy as there are no trees or vegetation. The facilities are the basic ones found in BC parks (fire pit, picnic table, firewood, pit toilets, water).

Recreational activities

The area is known for five hiking and back-country exploration trails accessed from the campground. These trails take up to a week to complete and let you appreciate the full beauty of this area of the Rocky Mountains. Summit Lake has a boat launch. Fishing for trout and whitefish in the lake and for arctic grayling and Dolly Varden in MacDonald Creek can be attempted. The fishing is not fantastic, however, as the waters are too cold to yield high fish populations. Mountaineering, horseback riding, photography, and wildlife observation are also available.

Additional information

This campground, located on the highest part of the Alaska Highway (1267 metres), is exposed to very cold winds. The scenery characterized by steep, bare mountain slopes is quite beautiful, and the location provides easy access into the back country. The park features erosion pillars and "hoodoos" plus sub-alpine lakes and waterfalls. One of the primary attractions of the area is the abundant wildlife, but visitors have to be patient in order to see the hundreds of mountain caribou, stone sheep, moose, mule deer, black and grizzly bear, lynx, wolverine, beaver, and elk that live in the region.

(courtesy BC Parks)

Swan Lake

Location

Swan Lake is probably the closest BC provincial park to the Alberta border and has a colourful history spreading over 50 years. The park is found 35 kilometres southeast of Dawson Creek on Highway 2, just north of Tupper, which has basic services. A one-kilometre gravel road leads to the campground. A comprehensive range of services is available at Dawson Creek.

Facilities

Situated on the lakeside there are 42 campsites catering to every type of recreational vehicle. There is no sani-station, limited access for the disabled, and facilities are restricted to the basic ones found in BC parks (fire pit, wood, water, picnic tables, pit toilets).

Recreational activities

Water-oriented activities are favoured at this location and include swimming from an excellent beach; fishing for northern pike, walleye, and perch; and boating on the five-kilometre Swan Lake. The park has a boat launch and water-skiing, and powerboats are permitted. Hikes around the lakeside can be taken from the campground. A large grassy area attracts day trippers and picnic parties, and there is an adventure playground for children as well as horseshoe pits and a baseball diamond.

Additional information

This 67-hectare park was established on 19 June 1918, making it BC's third oldest provincial park. It has a long record of hosting local social events and has been popular with residents of Dawson Creek for over 50 years. For those who are visiting the area for the first time, the town of Dawson Creek has an interesting pioneer village open during the summer months and worth a visit. Dawson Creek marks the start of the Alaska Highway: Mile 0.

Tetsa River

Location
If you crave fishing and tranquillity, this provincial park is for you. In the foothills of the Rocky Mountains at the meeting of the Tetsa River and Mill Creek, 100 kilometres west of Fort Nelson, is Tetsa River Provincial Park. The site is reached by travelling one kilometre along a gravel road off Highway 97. The nearest full range of services can be found at Fort Nelson.

Facilities
Twenty-five large, private campsites exist at this park. Approximately half overlook the water and many have grassed areas ideal for tents. All offer privacy and are set amid a poplar forest. There is no sani-station and only partial wheelchair accessibility. Facilities are confined to the basic camping ones (fire pit, wood, water, pit toilets, picnic tables).

Recreational activities
The main leisure pursuit here is fishing. As the Tetsa River flows into the Arctic drainage system, fishing for arctic grayling can be very rewarding in the spring and fall. It is also possible to take short strolls up and down the water's edge on a pebble beach area to explore the potential of other fishing locations.

Additional information
Tetsa River is one of the better BC parks geared primarily to overnight camping along the Alaska Highway because it offers private treed camping accommodation away from the main road. If you manage to stay in a site overlooking the river and enjoy fishing, this is a very quiet, beautiful location. When I visited, there were a number of people horseback riding in the area. The nearest large town is Fort Nelson. It is home of the Japanese-owned Canadian Chopstick Manufacturing Company Limited, the world's largest chopstick manufacturer, producing nine million pairs daily. The town also has a small museum close to the Visitor Centre which features information on the construction of the Alaska Highway.

Tudyah Lake

Location

A 56-hectare lakeside campground with a creek running through it awaits the weary traveller here. Tudyah Lake is found 157 kilometres from Prince George, at the southern end of Tudyah Lake in the Rocky Mountains between the Hart Ranges and the Nechako Plateau, close to the junction of Highway 97 and Highway 39. The nearest services are eight kilometres away at McLeod Lake.

Facilities

Primarily used for overnight stays, this campground has a somewhat unusual feel to it as the 36 sites are set in an open grassed meadow, giving a pleasant pastoral experience to camping. The spots are far enough apart to ensure privacy. There is no sani-station or access for the disabled, but the park includes all the basic amenities usually found (fire pit, wood, water, pit toilets, picnic tables).

Recreational activities

It is possible to swim, kayak, canoe, and fish at Tudyah Lake, and anglers should enjoy fishing for rainbow trout, Dolly Varden, and whitefish. There is a large group camping facility and day-use area with horseshoes. The town of Mackenzie, 30 minutes away, has a nine-hole golf course and a recreation centre, and is on the banks of Williston Lake, a prime fishing spot.

Additional information

The community of Mackenzie is at the south end of Williston Lake, a huge manmade reservoir which supplies water to the hydroelectric plant at Hudson's Hope. The town is named after Alexander Mackenzie, the first white person to reach Canada's Pacific coast by land. The town of Mackenzie was built in 1965 in an area of wilderness as a centre for pulp, paper, and lumber manufacturing. It has a museum and is home to the world's largest tree crusher, seen on the Mackenzie Boulevard, but it has little to commend it architecturally.

Whiskers Point

Location
Rich in native and pioneer history and situated on a sandspit jutting out into McLeod Lake, Whiskers Point is an extremely agreeable location to stop. The campground is 130 kilometres north of Prince George on Highway 97, about ten kilometres south of McLeod Lake, where gas, food, and lodging are available.

Facilities
Sixty-nine large secluded sites set in a mature forest of spruce and pine are available. A number of the campsites overlook the lake or are near Whiskers Creek, which runs through the campground. There is a sani-station, flush and pit toilets, and access for the disabled. Reservations are not accepted.

Recreational activities
McLeod Lake provides a wealth of opportunity for the water enthusiast. There is a good beach and excellent swimming; a concrete boat launch has been built; and fishing for Dolly Varden and rainbow trout occurs. (On a note of caution, the lake is subject to suddenly changing conditions, and strong winds can easily transform the calm water). For younger ones, a children's play area, horseshoes, and volleyball as well as a twenty-minute nature trail are available. The area is also rich in bird and animal life.

Additional information
I have visited Whiskers Point but have not spent a night here. All the literature on this area stresses the beauty of the sunsets visible from the park, which are described as "spectacular," "magnificent," and "breathtaking" in various publications. The community of McLeod Lake, ten kilometres to the north of the campground, was first established in 1805 by Simon Fraser (Fort McLeod) and was the first trading post and first European settlement west of the Rocky Mountains at the time. Although the Hart Highway (Highway 97) is a development of this century, the local Sekani people had a system of trails developed in this region long before the Europeans came. You will not be disappointed in your decision to stay here.

(courtesy BC Parks)

Camping Tours

The next chapter provides suggestions for one-, two-, and three-week camping excursions, originating in the Lower Mainland and designed for individuals travelling in a vehicle. The itineraries can easily be amended to accommodate personal preferences or alternative starting points. They act only as a recommendation for those who may not be too sure where they want to journey.

The following pages offer a brief synopsis of the roads on which it is necessary to travel for each of the recommended tours. These routes should be reviewed in conjunction with a detailed map of the province. A good map is required for anyone planning to camp and travel in BC. One such map is *The British Columbia Recreational Atlas*. An excellent resource, it provides comprehensive, detailed coverage of all the major and minor routes as well as data on places, area boundaries, trails, elevations, lakes, and parks. The fact that it is an 11" by 8" bound map *book* and not a four foot by four foot paper map makes it easy to read in the car (and to keep in one piece). In addition, Super Natural British Columbia distributes a *Parks Guide and Road Map* which numerically lists all provincial parks. Both these publications are readily available at tourist information offices while the *Recreational Atlas* is carried in most book stores.

For those who may be uncomfortable travelling without a reservation, each of the one-, two-, and three-week tours has a "fully reserved" option where it is possible to book all camping spots in advance. Anyone planning to vacation in the popular peak months of July and August without a reservation must be prepared to come across some full campgrounds and to plan alternative options.

Seven-Day Tours

Trip 1: A Little Taste of the Province

Although this route may seem to involve a lot of driving, for those who like this pastime it provides a good introduction to the province, a taste of some of the best scenery, and an introduction to lovely provincial parks. It encompasses a circular tour travelling north to Highway 97, east on the Yellowhead Highway, south on Highway 93, then west on Highway 3.

Day 1	Lac la Hache	Day 5	Moyie Lake
Day 2	Mount Robson	Day 6	Kettle River
Day 3	Mount Robson	Day 7	Manning
Day 4	Kootenay National Park		

Trip 2: Fully Reserved

This itinerary gives campers the security of knowing they have accommodation in some of the most popular campgrounds in the province. It also utilizes campgrounds on the BC Mainland, Vancouver Island, and the Gulf Islands necessitating wonderful ferry trips and minimal driving. After staying at Alice Lake, travel south on the Sea to Sky Highway to Horseshoe Bay and take the ferry to Vancouver Island. From there it is just a short drive north on Highway 19 to Rathtrevor. After Rathtrevor head south on Highway 19 to Goldstream. To reach Montague Harbour take a ferry from Swartz Bay to Galiano Island.

Day 1	Alice Lake	Day 5	Goldstream
Day 2	Alice Lake	Day 6	Montague Harbour
Day 3	Rathtrevor	Day 7	Montague Harbour
Day 4	Rathtrevor		

As you tour our province watch for birds such as this Canada Jay.
(courtesy Al Nickull)

Camping Tours

Trip 3: Vancouver Island and Island Hopping

Like Tour 2, this route has some fantastic ferry rides through breathtaking scenery. Montague Harbour on Galiano Island is reached by ferry from Tsawwassen. Ruckle Provincial Park is on Saltspring Island, and ferries regularly leave from Galiano for Saltspring. From Saltspring, take a ferry to Swartz Bay; from here the Island Highway leads to Goldstream and Bamberton. French Beach is located south of Victoria on Highway 14.

Day 1	Montague Harbour	Day 5	Goldstream
Day 2	Montague Harbour	Day 6	Bamberton
Day 3	Ruckle	Day 7	French Beach
Day 4	Ruckle		

Trip 4: Circle Tour

This easy-to-complete circular excursion takes campers to some of the less popular camping spots easily accessible from Vancouver. It involves driving north on the lovely Sea to Sky Highway, Highway 99, then (after a brief diversion off Route 99 to access Birkenhead), continuing along this scenic road until it joins Highway 97 just north of Cache Creek. At Cache Creek take Highway 97C south to Kentucky Alleyne. From this campground travel south on Highway 5A to Highway 3, which leads through Manning Park back to Vancouver.

Day 1	Nairn Falls	Day 5	Manning
Day 2	Birkenhead	Day 6	Manning
Day 3	Birkenhead	Day 7	Emory
Day 4	Kentucky-Alleyne		

Trip 5: The Hiker's Dream

This trip is designed for driving one day and hiking the next. To reach Wells Gray take the Coquihalla toll road (Highway 5) to Kamloops and then Highway 5 north. After Wells Gray continue north on Highway 5 until it joins the Yellowhead Highway (Route 16). After Mount Robson take the fantastic Glacier Highway (Highway 93) south until it meets Highway 1. (Pray for good weather as the views along this road are some of the best in the province.) Travelling west on Highway 1 leads to Yoho. From Yoho it is possible to drive back to Vancouver in a day. For those who want a less hurried route, my advice would be to take Highway 1 as far as Kamloops, then Highway 97 until it reaches Highway 99 and return to Vancouver on Highway 99.

Day 1	Wells Gray	Day 5	Yoho
Day 2	Wells Gray	Day 6	Yoho
Day 3	Mount Robson	Day 7	Marble Canyon
Day 4	Mount Robson		

Fourteen-Day Tours

Trip 1: A Bigger Taste of the Province

Two weeks is a good time period in which to plan a camping tour of the province. Minimal driving is undertaken on the first day of this itinerary as campers head out of Vancouver on Highway 7 to Golden Ears. After camping here, continue on Highway 7 until the junction with Highway 3 is reached, then take Highway 3 through Manning. After Manning, travel north to Kamloops. A number of routes are available, but my advice for those who have time is to take 5A. From Kamloops take Route 5 north until it joins the Yellowhead Highway. Travel east on the Yellowhead until Highway 93, which can be taken all the way south to Kootenay National Park and beyond, where it meets route 95. From Jimsmith Lake follow Highway 3, then 3A to Crawford Bay (and the longest free ferry ride in the world) over the Kootenay Lake where Highway 31 leads to Kootenay Lake Provincial Park. Travel south from Kootenay Lake on Highway 3A and take a slow drive along Route 3 back to Vancouver.

Day 1	Golden Ears	Day 8	Mount Robson
Day 2	Manning	Day 9	Kootenay National Park
Day 3	Manning	Day 10	Kootenay National Park
Day 4	Paul Lake	Day 11	Jimsmith Lake
Day 5	Wells Gray	Day 12	Kootenay Lake
Day 6	Wells Gray	Day 13	Kootenay Lake
Day 7	Mount Robson	Day 14	Haynes Point

Trip 2: Fully Reserved

This excursion utilizes campgrounds which accept reservations. It also is recommended for families (who may want to cut out the northern excursion to Mount Robson). Travel along Route 7 to Highway 3 and continue east on this road until it meets Highway 97. At this juncture you will adopt a northward direction as the road leads towards Highway 1, dividing into Highways 97, 97A and 97B. All these roads lead in the direction of Shuswap Lake. After staying at Shuswap Lake, drive west on Highway 1 to Kamloops, then take Route 5 north to the Yellowhead Highway and the stunningly beautiful Robson Park. Retrace your steps back to Kamloops and follow Highway 5A south to Princeton and the nearby Otter Lake Provincial Park. The return journey to Vancouver leads you back on Highway 3.

Day 1	Golden Ears	Day 8	Shuswap Lake
Day 2	Golden Ears	Day 9	Shuswap Lake
Day 3	Manning	Day 10	Shuswap Lake
Day 4	Manning	Day 11	Mount Robson
Day 5	Okanagan Lake	Day 12	Mount Robson
Day 6	Okanagan Lake	Day 13	Mount Robson
Day 7	Okanagan Lake	Day 14	Otter Lake

Camping Tours

Trip 3: Vancouver Island and Gulf Island Hopping

On this lovely relaxed excursion you will be able to explore all the camping highlights of Vancouver Island and the Gulf islands. Montague Harbour on Galiano Island is reached by ferry from Tsawwassen. Ruckle Provincial Park is on Saltspring Island, and ferries regularly leave from Galiano for Saltspring. From Saltspring, a ferry is needed to reach South Pender Island, the last Gulf Island on the tour. Travel from South Pender Island to Vancouver Island's Swartz Bay by ferry. At Swartz Bay the Island Highway (Route 1) leads south to Victoria. Take Highway 14 from Victoria to French Beach. From here the return journey north starts, utilizing the Island Highway to drive as far as Parksville. At Parksville head west on Highway 4, meandering across Vancouver Island to Pacific Rim National Park (the road from Port Alberni to the coast is particularly lovely). Return along this road back to the Island Highway and continue north until reaching Campbell River. Highway 28 just north of this town leads into Strathcona Park. Return to the Lower Mainland by ferry leaving from Nanaimo.

Day 1	Montague Harbour	Day 8	Bamberton
Day 2	Montague Harbour	Day 9	Pacific Rim
Day 3	Ruckle	Day 10	Pacific Rim
Day 4	Ruckle	Day 11	Miracle Beach
Day 5	Prior Centennial	Day 12	Strathcona
Day 6	French Beach	Day 13	Strathcona
Day 7	Goldstream	Day 14	Strathcona

Take time to do some beachcombing—you may find treasures like this "sand collar," the egg case of a moon snail. (courtesy Al Nickull)

Trip 4: Fruit and Freedom—The Okanagan and the Kootenays

This tour offers the best of both worlds, as the somewhat more populated Okanagan is visited in conjunction with the calm, quiet Kootenays. The quickest way to reach Bear Creek, the first provincial park campground on the itinerary, is to take Highway 1 out of Vancouver then the Coquihalla Highway ($10.00 toll road) to Merritt and turn east on Highway 97C towards Kelowna. Alternatively, do not use the Coquihalla and instead take Highway 3 through Manning Park to Princeton, then Highway 5A north to Highway 97. From Bear Creek drive north to Vernon, then take Highway 6 east to reach Mabel Lake. After staying here, continue on Route 6 until the turnoff for Highway 31A is met; this leads to Highway 31, and by travelling north, to Kootenay Lake Provincial Park. From Kootenay Lake, travel south on Highway 31 and take Highway 3A to find Kokanee Creek. A short drive south on this road leads to Champion Lakes. Continue the journey back to Vancouver on Route 3, stopping at Otter Lake and Manning or other campgrounds which look appealing.

Day 1	Bear Creek	Day 8	Kootenay Lake
Day 2	Bear Creek	Day 9	Kokanee Creek
Day 3	Mabel Lake	Day 10	Champion Lakes
Day 4	Mabel Lake	Day 11	Otter Lake
Day 5	Rosebery	Day 12	Otter Lake
Day 6	Kootenay Lake	Day 13	Manning
Day 7	Kootenay Lake	Day 14	Manning

Trip 5: Rocky Mountains and the National Parks

It is easily possible to visit all the "big" parks in a two-week period, but a few long days in the car are required. This tour has been designed to compensate for these long travelling times with two- or three-night stays in some of the largest and most spectacular parks in the province. To take this excursion, leave Vancouver on Highway 1, then take the Coquihalla toll road ($10.00) north to Kamloops. Just north of Kamloops is Paul Lake Provincial Park. The following day take Route 1 east to Glacier, and a few days later proceed the few kilometres to Yoho. From Yoho, Route 1 east leads to Lake Louise. From here, head south on Highway 93 to Kootenay National Park. Continue on Route 93, which eventually becomes Route 95 and joins Route 3. Route 3 travels across the bottom of the province and leads back to Vancouver.

Day 1	Paul Lake	Day 8	Kootenay National Park
Day 2	Glacier	Day 9	Kootenay National Park
Day 3	Glacier	Day 10	Kootenay National Park
Day 4	Glacier	Day 11	Moyie Lake
Day 5	Yoho	Day 12	Kettle River
Day 6	Yoho	Day 13	Manning
Day 7	Yoho	Day 14	Manning

Camping Tours

Twenty-One-Day Tours

Trip 1: A Huge Taste of the Province

If travelling hundreds of kilometres a day across remote regions of the province is a pleasurable notion for you, then this trip will be a dream. I undertook it in 19 days, which required a lot of driving—over 6,500 kilometres. It is not an itinerary for those who suffer from motion sickness. Leave Vancouver on the Sea to Sky Highway and travel north on what I believe to be one of the best roads in the world. When the road joins Highway 97, head north. This is the Gold Rush Trail. After stopping at Lac La Hache and turning east just north of Quesnel on Highway 26 to visit Barkerville, return to Highway 97 and proceed north to Prince George. From here, turn west on the Yellowhead Highway (Highway 16). At Terrace, take Highway 97 south to Lakelse, after which you should be prepared to travel north on this highway as far as the Alaska Highway. (Be warned that sections of Highway 37 between Dease Lake and Meziadin Junction are unpaved.) Upon reaching the Alaska Highway, head south as far as Dawson Creek, then drive Route 97 south to Prince George. At Prince George, travel east on the Yellowhead Highway to Mount Robson, then head south on Highway 5 to Kamloops. At Kamloops you can choose between returning to Vancouver via the fast Coquihalla toll road or Route 1 through the Fraser Canyon.

Day 1	Lac la Hache
Day 2	Barkerville
Day 3	Barkerville
Day 4	Sowchea Bay
Day 5	Sowchea Bay
Day 6	Tyhee Lake
Day 7	Lakelse Lake
Day 8	Lakelse Lake
Day 9	Meziadin Lake
Day 10	Boya Lake
Day 11	Liard River
Day 12	Liard River
Day 13	Buckinghorse
Day 14	Gwillim Lake
Day 15	Bear Lake
Day 16	Bear Lake
Day 17	Mount Robson
Day 18	Mount Robson
Day 19	Wells Gray
Day 20	Wells Gray
Day 21	Emory Creek

Horseback riding can be a pleasant way to explore.
(courtesy Darlene Nickull)

Provincial and National Park Campgrounds in BC

Trip 2: Fully Reserved

Many of the campgrounds detailed in this itinerary are ideal for families and for those who require more comfort when camping (for example flush toilets, showers, and nearby stores). To reach the first campground leave Vancouver on Highway 1, then take Highway 3, which meanders through Manning Park. Carry on travelling east along this road until you reach Osoyoos, then head north on Highway 97. After staying at Ellison continue the journey north on Highway 97 until you meet the junction with Highway 1. At this stage head west as far as Kamloops, then north on Highway 5 to the Yellowhead Highway and Mount Robson. After Mount Robson take the Yellowhead Highway west to Prince George, then travel north on Highway 97 as far as Crooked River. On the next stage of the journey, take Route 97 south as far as the turn for Highway 99, just north of Cache Creek. You will spend the final days of your camping tour driving the wonderful Highway 99 back to Vancouver.

Day 1	Manning	Day 12	Crooked River
Day 2	Manning	Day 13	Crooked River
Day 3	Manning	Day 14	Barkerville
Day 4	Okanagan Lake	Day 15	Barkerville
Day 5	Okanagan Lake	Day 16	Green Lake
Day 6	Okanagan Lake	Day 17	Green Lake
Day 7	Ellison	Day 18	Green Lake
Day 8	Ellison	Day 19	Alice Lake
Day 9	Mount Robson	Day 20	Alice Lake
Day 10	Mount Robson	Day 21	Porteau Cove
Day 11	Mount Robson		

Trip 3: Vancouver Island, Gulf Islands, and the Sunshine Coast

An easy-to-complete excursion featuring beautiful drives and numerous ferry rides, this route follows the same one as detailed above in the 14-day Vancouver Island and Gulf Island Hopping (see above). However, upon leaving Strathcona Provincial Park, travellers extend their tour by taking the ferry from Courtenay to Powell River on the Sunshine Coast. From here, drive south on Highway 101. To end the journey, take the ferry back to Horseshoe Bay.

Day 1	Montague Harbour	Day 12	Pacific Rim
Day 2	Montague Harbour	Day 13	Pacific Rim
Day 3	Ruckle	Day 14	Miracle Beach
Day 4	Ruckle	Day 15	Strathcona
Day 5	Prior Centennial	Day 16	Strathcona
Day 6	Goldstream	Day 17	Strathcona
Day 7	Goldstream	Day 18	Saltery Bay
Day 8	Bamberton	Day 19	Saltery Bay
Day 9	Rathtrevor	Day 20	Porpoise Cove
Day 10	Rathtrevor	Day 21	Porpoise Cove
Day 11	Pacific Rim		

Trip 4: Gold Rush Trail and the Queen Charlotte Islands

The drawback of this trip is that the same roads have to be travelled on the outward and the return journey. However, reaching the Queen Charlotte Islands and the scenery en route more than compensate for this requirement. From Vancouver, go north via Highways 99 and 97 as far as Prince George, then follow the Yellowhead Highway west to Prince Rupert, where a six-hour ferry ride connects you to the Queen Charlottes. Retrace the same route back until just north of Cache Creek, where you can continue the Gold Rush Trail south (Highway 1) down the Fraser Canyon all the way to Hope.

Day 1	Lac la Hache	Day 12	Naikoon
Day 2	Sowchea	Day 13	Naikoon
Day 3	Sowchea	Day 14	Exchamsiks River
Day 4	Tyhee Lake	Day 15	Beaumont
Day 5	Lakelse Lake	Day 16	Beaumont
Day 6	Lakelse Lake	Day 17	Barkerville
Day 7	Lakelse Lake	Day 18	Barkerville
Day 8	Prudhomme Lake	Day 19	Green Lake
Day 9	Naikoon	Day 20	Green Lake
Day 10	Naikoon	Day 21	Emory Creek
Day 11	Naikoon		

Trip 5: The Rockies and the Larger Provincial and National Parks

Designed with the hiker in mind, this itinerary features some of the best parks in the province. On leaving Vancouver take either Route 1 or the quieter Route 7 to the junction of Highway 3. Travel east on Highway 3 to Castlegar, then Route 3A to Kokanee Creek. Continue along Route 3A until it rejoins Highway 3, which turns into Highway 95 and leads north into Kootenay National Park. Next travel north to meet Highway 1, then drive west through Yoho and Glacier National Parks as far as Kamloops, where Route 5 leads north to the Yellowhead Highway and Mount Robson. From Mount Robson head west on Route 16 (the Yellowhead Highway) as far as Prince George and then south on Highway 97, back through the Fraser Canyon to Vancouver.

Day 1	Manning	Day 12	Glacier
Day 2	Manning	Day 13	Glacier
Day 3	Kokanee Creek	Day 14	Wells Gray
Day 4	Kokanee Creek	Day 15	Wells Gray
Day 5	Moyie Lake	Day 16	Wells Gray
Day 6	Kootenay National Park	Day 17	Mount Robson
Day 7	Kootenay National Park	Day 18	Mount Robson
Day 8	Kootenay National Park	Day 19	Mount Robson
Day 9	Yoho	Day 20	Ten Mile Lake
Day 10	Yoho	Day 21	Downing
Day 11	Yoho		

Author Jayne Seagrave enjoys exploring Kootenay National Park.

Jayne Seagrave lives in East Vancouver with her husband, Andrew. She holds a Ph.D. in Criminology and divides her time between: teaching at Simon Fraser University; researching policy issues; helping her husband with the marketing of his small business; and camping, travelling and exploring the province of British Columbia.

OUR NEXT EDITION WILL INCLUDE READER TIPS AND RECOMMENDATIONS. PLEASE E-MAIL COMMENTS TO OUR EDITORIAL OFFICE AT herhouse@island.net.